EXPLORERS

Discovering the World through the Study of Five Great Lives

FROM THE CREATIVE LIVES SERIES

by

Chris Brewer, M.A.

ZEPHYR PRESS
Tucson, Arizona

EXPLORERS
Discovering the World through
the Study of Five Great Lives

Grades 3–8

ISBN 0-913705-78-0

Cover Art: Michelle Gallardo
Editors: Stacey Lynn and Stacey Shropshire
Book Design, Production and some Illustration: Nancy Taylor

Zephyr Press
P.O. Box 13448
Tucson, Arizona 85732-3448

CONTENTS

*D*edicated with love to my children, May and David Brewer, with whom I plan to have many more "great explores."

With special appreciation to Edgar Mitchell for sharing his personal experience and in honor of his insight and clarity into the needs of our time; to the Cousteau Society and NASA for their assistance in developing this study guide; to the Flathead County Library and the Flathead Valley Community College Library for endless interlibrary loans; to Rod Brewer for his insight and assistance; to Ted Boyd, Ellen Boyd, and Ken Brewer for sharing their spirit of adventure and for the memories of journeys into the unknown.

I INTRODUCTION

Students turn to models not for definition but for direction; if no positive models are made available, students often choose the first image they encounter. Because young people are preparing for a world full of difficult and sometimes threatening choices, we need to ask ourselves these questions: How does a teacher present great minds and souls to students and at the same time elicit their commitment to discover their own unique voices? How does a teacher offer an example of human potential that doesn't encourage mere mimicry? Where does the courage to discover and realize our own destinies come from?

These were some of the concerns that influenced our choices when we compiled this guide. We selected several explorers based on their deep desire to know and understand the world. Although these individuals explored different regions of the world, all were responding to the human need to grow. Their experiences have a message for us that can cross the boundaries of culture, space, and time, and we hope that some of their spirit comes through these pages.

The Philosophy of This Guide

Education can be a quest to know oneself. Therefore, a study of explorers should be more than a look into their lives. Though much can be gained by understanding the strength and individuality of these explorers, the challenge lies in eliciting the courage students need to excel as individuals. The biographical sketches, descriptions of explorations, and extended reading are intended to facilitate students' growth. The many activities in this book can provide knowledge and understanding of the explorers' lives and expand each student's awareness of the meaning and role of exploration in the human experience. More important, students can use the activities to encourage their own natural curiosity and to develop deeper insight into their sense of self and personal goals.

Through a variety of activities, this guide involves all of the intelligences: musical, logical-mathematical, linguistic, spatial, bodily-kinesthetic, intrapersonal, and interpersonal.[1] The activities creatively expand cognitive, affective, and psychomotor skills. Bloom's Taxonomy of Cognitive Objectives, Krathwohl's Taxonomy of Affective Objectives, and Simpson's Taxonomy of Psychomotor Objectives have been implemented throughout the guide. The integration of thinking, feeling, and doing into creative learning experiences ensures greater opportunity for a teacher to educate by drawing forth rather than leading. Your active involvement, enthusiasm, and insight will also make the process more alive for students.

Taxonomy of Objectives[2]

THINKING: Taxonomy of Cognitive Objectives

Knowledge ....learning the information

Comprehension.....................understanding the meaning of the material

Application ....applying the information

Analysis ....analyzing the parts to understand their structure

Synthesis ....seeing the whole picture and developing creative insights

Evaluation ....judging the value of the material

FEELING: Taxonomy of Affective Objectives

Receiving...............................attending to an event or stimuli

Responding ....participating actively in the learning event

Valuing..................................placing value on the event or object

Organizing ....bringing together different values, resolving conflicts between them, and building an internal value system

Characterizing ....acting consistently in accordance with an internal value system

DOING: Taxonomy of Psychomotor Objectives

Perception ....being aware of materials and methods of use

Set ....demonstrating mental and physical readiness for projects

Guided Response ....beginning to learn skills through imitation and exploration

Mechanism ....gaining confidence and facility through habit and practice in skills

Complex Overt Response.......gaining skill and ease in performing activities

Adaptation ....modifying learned techniques for adaptation to various situations

Origination ....creating new techniques and ideas to fit a particular situation

Learner Outcomes

- To comprehend the importance of human exploration

- To gain knowledge of the role of exploration in this culture and other cultures, past and contemporary

- To understand that an explorer's journey reflects the needs and goals of society

- To discover that exploration is an essential part of learning and living for a society and individuals

- To identify the emotional, physical, mental, and spiritual aspects of exploration

- To recognize the personal qualities that are characteristic of great explorers

- To appreciate the combination of creative thought process, analytical reasoning skills, and personal determination that are necessary in any form of exploration

- To develop personal curiosity and exploratory skills as tools for learning and living

- To find ways to make use of the exploration process, both at home and at school

- To realize that intrapersonal exploration provides individuals with a better understanding of their needs and goals so they may confidently move into exploration of the outer world

Using This Guide

Explorers are sometimes considered unique individuals with special qualities. But exploration and discovery are natural processes that are present in all aspects of living and learning. When nurtured and developed, the traits of curiosity, determination, self-confidence, creativity, and reasoning can help the student build a fulfilling life. Some of the best examples of explorers are the children whose boundless curiosity leads them to freely experience and question the wonders of the world around them. In this guide we seek to encourage appreciation of important explorers, to preserve the joy of self-discovery, and to provide opportunities for personal expression and active experience.

Explorers is a learning center within a book. It contains biographies of five explorers as well as activities to develop exploration skills and to encourage curiosity. Its generous reference list (p. 93) contains rich resources written for both children and adults. We hope you'll add your own resources: posters, videos, and artifacts that will excite your students. Designate a special section of the classroom as a learning center with chairs, tables, resources, and bulletin boards; provide ample time for browsing.

Reproduce the student-directed activities in the explorers' sections and glue each assignment to a piece of colored tagboard that has been cut into a shape to fit the subject: a ship, a continent, or a shape your students create. Decide how many of the assignments each student should complete, then let students select their own assignments based on their personal interest and enthusiasm. There is value in giving students the opportunity to read and consider all the assignments and then choose their own. They will learn as they read, perhaps find a new interest or direction to pursue, and develop independent learning skills. Here are some specific guidelines for using this book:

- The goal of this guide is to stimulate students to process information using higher levels of thinking and creativity. A basic knowledge of the material and a creative environment are essential.

- The cognitive, affective, and psychomotor objectives are all hierarchical models. Each skill level builds on the previous one. Requiring students to complete an activity at each level is not necessary if you employ some means to ensure they have the necessary understanding of the material.

- Read through the activities and check for skills that will need special attention and direction.

- Find vocabulary words that are important to the study of explorers but will be new for your students. Have students learn the new words by making crossword puzzles or creating other vocabulary activities.

- The activities are designed to provide experiences in the various intelligences, as defined by Howard Gardner. Encourage students to work within each intelligence, to expand their personal learning styles, and to explore various modes of expression. An explorer is a risk taker.

- One way to evaluate student progress is to develop general criteria based on district and program goals for all students, and then to allow each student to develop his or her additional criteria for evaluation with the help of the teacher and perhaps a parent. When possible, the evaluation should include people other than the teacher and the student. Other school personnel or community members may assist in some aspects.

Facilitating the Learning Experience

In self-directed units, the teacher is a resource person, a co-facilitator on the student's discovery and learning journey. One of the most important tasks within this role is to provide a nurturing and stimulating environment that encourages learning and is relatively free of stress. Such an environment includes:

- A variety of materials and references
- Time and freedom to explore
- Opportunities for new experiences
- Psychological safety and freedom
- Encouragement of self-reliance and determination
- Valuing of the creative process

Notes
1. See Howard Gardner, *Frames of Mind: The Theory of Multiple Intelligences* (New York: Basic Books, 1983).
2. Adapted from Benjamin S. Bloom, et al., *Taxonomy of Educational Objectives, Handbook 1: Cognitive Domain* (New York; David McKay, 1956). Also see Norman E. Gronlund, *How to Write and Use Instructional Objectives* (New York: Macmillan, 1991).

Edgar Mitchell

Mary Kingsley

Jacques-Yves Cousteau

Christopher Columbus

Roald Amundsen

II
THE EXPLORERS

Christopher Columbus
1451–1506

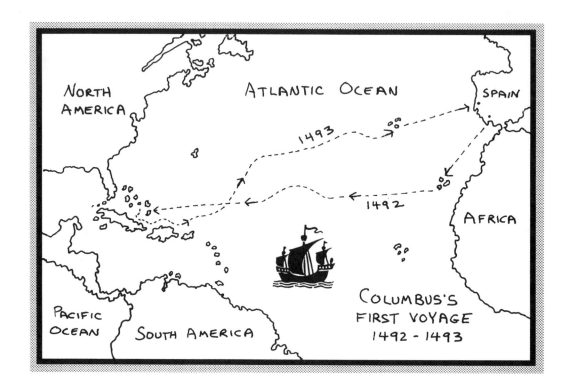

North America

Atlantic Ocean

Spain

1493

1492

Africa

Pacific Ocean

South America

Columbus's First Voyage 1492 - 1493

Overview

Christopher Columbus, like many explorers before him, challenged the ideas of his time. He had the will, determination, and creativity to seek answers to questions about Earth's geography, and his journeys paved the way for other explorers and settlers. The result was an important meeting of world cultures that changed the lives of people on both sides of the ocean forever. Although positive changes occurred, Columbus and the Europeans who followed him can be criticized for their ill treatment of the people whose land they took. The Europeans terrorized and enslaved the native people and took their gold and other valuables. Thousands of Native Americans died and entire cultures were lost.

Looking back on these events, however, we can gain insight into the past and recognize the mistakes of the eager newcomers. We can learn about relationships between cultures and carefully choose our actions toward one another in the future. By using the same courage and conviction that explorers such as Columbus have shown, we can create a "new world"—one that honors and provides for the needs of Earth and her diverse cultures.

Early Years

Christopher Columbus, Christoforo Columbo, Christouon Collon, Cristobal Colon, Joan Bautista Colom, Johannes Scolvus, Jan of Kovno—which one was the sea captain who crossed the Ocean Sea (Atlantic Ocean) in 1492? And was he Genoese, Portuguese, Spanish, Croatian, Norwegian, Jewish? Had he been a wool weaver, a map maker, a pirate, a sailor, a nobleman?

Mystery surrounds the early life of Christopher Columbus, and we may never know all the facts. Most people believe the account that says Christopher Columbus was born Cristobal Colon in Genoa in 1451. He was the son of a weaver and learned his father's trade, but soon became restless and entered life on the sea. He received no education as a child but later learned to read and write in Latin, Spanish, Italian, and Portuguese.

Columbus is said to have been taller than average with blue eyes, freckles, and reddish hair that turned gray and then white at an early age. Some said his manner allowed others to "look on him with love." Although he could be quite charming, he could also be very quiet and sometimes had trouble communicating. On occasion he was demanding and impatient.

Around 1470 Columbus married Felipa Perestrello e Moniz, the daughter of a deceased Portuguese ship captain and colonial official. Felipa's mother gave Columbus her late husband's maps, logs, and navigation charts, which contained a great deal of information on currents, wind patterns, landmarks, and ocean conditions.

The young couple settled on Porto Santo in the Madeira Islands and had one child named Diego. In 1483 they moved to Portugal, but two years later Felipa became ill and died. Columbus took his young son to Spain. There, Columbus became friends with Father Antonio Marchena of the Franciscan monastery, who was very interested in nautical studies and Columbus's ideas about sailing the Ocean Sea. Diego stayed at the monastery as a student. Later Columbus fell in love with Beatriz Enriques de Harana, with whom he had a second son.

At that time, people were sailing to the Indies over a route discovered by Portuguese explorer Bartolomeu Dias. But Columbus was convinced that the Indies could also be reached by sailing west across the Ocean Sea. He studied many books about the oceans, science, and navigation. He kept a copy of the *Imago Mundi (Images of the World)* with him on all his voyages and wrote many notes about ocean geography in it. He also read many geography, philosophy, and mathematics books. Columbus was especially interested in Marco Polo's accounts of his travels and the twenty years he spent in the Orient.

Columbus made his own charts and calculations to prove he could sail west to the Indies from Spain. He used information from the many books he read to support his theory. He even used the Bible to prove that the Indies must be close. Most people in the 1400s believed Earth was round and the Indies lay west across the Ocean Sea. But they also thought it was so far to the Indies that no ship could carry enough provisions for the crew to survive the long journey. Actually, they were right. Ten thousand miles lay between Columbus's last port in the Canary Islands and the Indies—too far for a ship in the 1400s to travel without stopping for more supplies. However, between Europe and the Indies lay the Americas, and the 2,400 miles between the continents can be traveled in as little as three or four weeks.

Columbus believed he was the explorer who would successfully sail across the Ocean Sea to the Indies. A deeply religious man, he felt it was God's will that he make the voyage. But he spent seven years trying to find someone to provide him with the ships and supplies he would need for the journey. He approached the governments of Portugal, Spain, England, and France for their assistance. However, his idea was so unusual that he could not convince anyone to take the risk of financing him. A committee of learned men studied the issue for Queen Isabella of Spain and even they concluded the journey was impossible.

But the idea interested the Spanish royalty, who desperately wanted to find their own ocean trade route to the Indies in order to make their country rich. In addition, Queen Isabella and King Ferdinand were devout Catholics who were determined to spread the Catholic religion. Gold, glory, and God were said to have been the reasons that they eventually supported the voyages of Columbus.

The First Voyage: 1492–1493

On April 17, 1492, King Ferdinand and Queen Isabella signed an agreement to give Christopher Columbus titles and wealth if he successfully reached the Indies. They also wrote a letter of introduction to the rulers of the foreign land they hoped Columbus would find.

The king and queen ordered the expedition to be outfitted in a small harbor town called Palos. The town was to provide three fully equipped vessels within one month, but finding a crew and outfitting the ships took three and a half months. Martín and Vicente Pinzón, who were well-known, trusted citizens of Palos as well as able seamen, donated two of their own ships, the *Niña* and the *Pinta,* for the venture and served as commanders aboard them. The *Niña* and the *Pinta* were caravels, a type of ship designed for exploration by the Portuguese explorer Prince Henry the Navigator. They were smaller than the awkward trading ships that were built to haul as much cargo as possible.

The people of Palos did not know Columbus well but the men joined the crew because they trusted the Pinzóns. The king and queen's order had stated that if necessary, criminals could be pardoned for their crimes if they made the voyage with Columbus, but of the ninety men who were taken as crew, only four were criminals. Most were able seamen, but there were also carpenters, servants, a surgeon, a silversmith, and several boys who had never been to sea. All of the crew except Columbus and four others were Spanish. On August 3 the ships were ready to sail.

Columbus began the voyage by sailing south to the Canary Islands because he believed the Indies were on the same latitude. On the 800-mile journey, the *Pinta* developed rudder problems that had to be repaired before leaving the islands. On September 9 the ships again raised their sails and headed west across the Ocean Sea to look for the Indies.

As the ships left at dusk, the sailors watched the land disappear and must have wondered if they would ever return. Columbus knew his men were afraid. He kept a log of the journey, but he also kept a private journal in which he recorded the miles he estimated the ships had traveled. In the log he recorded fewer miles so the crews would be less nervous about how far they had traveled without finding land.

The crews became even more nervous about the voyage when the ships drifted into the Sargasso Sea, an area of the Atlantic Ocean that is covered with a thick, floating seaweed called sargassum. The seaweed covers miles of water and makes the entire ocean surface look yellowish green. The seamen had never seen such a sight and were afraid of being trapped by the seaweed. Finally, huge waves moved the ships toward the west into clear waters.

The *Santa Maria,* the largest of the three vessels, was only about seventy-eight feet long. She carried forty men and boys as crew. The ships were crowded and the crew slept in shifts, sometimes fighting just for a place to sleep on the deck. They had one hot meal a day, which they ate from wooden bowls with their fingers. The food carried by the ships included wine, water, salted meat and sardines, cheese, chick-peas, lentils, beans, rice, oil, honey, vinegar, garlic, almonds, raisins, and special biscuits called hardtack.

There were no accurate tools for measuring distances in the 1400s, but Columbus seemed particularly gifted in understanding the sea. He determined his course by dead reckoning, a method sailors used to calculate their location by guessing a ship's speed and keeping track of the direction it was traveling with a magnetic compass. Recent evaluations of Columbus's figures reveal that his records were nearly correct.

The ships sailed day and night, with the sailors taking turns running the ships on four-hour watches. The watches were timed by a half-hour sandglass, which the ships' boys turned over each time the sand had filtered into the bottom. The sailors' anxious eyes would scan the horizon for land. Twice someone thought he saw land and cried out "Land ho!" only to be disappointed. It was not surprising that the crews began to talk of turning back. After a month at sea the men's grumbling began to get louder. The crews talked among themselves about throwing Columbus into the sea and returning to Spain. They would tell Ferdinand and Isabella that Columbus had fallen overboard.

A meeting of the Pinzón brothers and Columbus was held; the ships' commanders all agreed that their crews wanted to return home. Columbus refused to turn around but promised that if they had not reached land in two or three days he would order the ships home. He also agreed to change course as Martín Pinzón had suggested and sail more to the southwest, the direction from which they had recently seen flocks of birds flying.

The next day signs began to appear that suggested Columbus was right about being close to land: a reed floated past the *Santa Maria,* the crew of the *Niña* picked up a green branch with a flower on it, and the crew of the *Pinta* found a stick that looked as if it had been carved.

The men sang "Salve Regina" to end the day and that night Columbus thought he saw a light on the water. But in the morning there was no sign of land. The day passed uneventfully. Then at 2 A.M. the following morning the shout of "Land ho!" again sounded. This time it brought tears to the eyes of the relieved crew, for there, indeed, was land.

The ships dropped anchor and the crews waited until daylight to go ashore. Few slept, and as dawn broke they eagerly began to look for a landing site. By noon Columbus found a small bay and put the launches in the water. As Columbus and his officers set foot on land, they fell to their knees and kissed the earth. The explorers gave thanks to the Lord, displayed their Spanish banners, and planted a large cross in the soil. Columbus claimed the land for Spain, ignoring the rights of the people who already lived in this land. He chose to name the island San Salvador, which means Holy Savior in Spanish.

The first meeting between the native peoples and Columbus was peaceful. The copper-colored natives thought the mysterious white men must be from heaven. Feeling sure he had indeed found the East Indies, Columbus called the natives "Indians." Marco Polo had written that the people of the Indies dressed in silk and gold. Columbus was surprised that the natives were "quite naked as their mothers bore them" except for the paint some put on their faces and bodies.

Columbus had landed not in the East Indies, as he imagined, but on the Bahama Islands in what is today called the West Indies. The land he saw was enchanting, with lush tropical plants, flocks of parrots and other brightly colored birds, and a delicious fragrance in the air. He thought this might be the beautiful land of riches called Cipangu (Japan) that Marco Polo described. However, the native people lived in thatched huts, had few belongings, and ate only the vegetables they grew and the cassava bread they baked. To Columbus, these people seemed simple and gentle. He wrote in his log that he thought they could be easily overpowered and made slaves for Spain.

Though the explorers and natives could not speak each others' language, they communicated by making hand signs. Columbus wanted to win the people's trust and gave them small trinkets—glass beads, mirrors, and bells. The islanders gave the mysterious newcomers food, parrots, woven cloth, and pieces of pottery. Few of the natives had any gold or valuables, but they seemed to be telling Columbus that gold could be found in the area.

The inhabitants spoke of Colba (Cuba) and Cubanacan (city of Cuba). Thinking he was hearing of Cipangu and Kublai Khan, Columbus explored the islands looking for Japan and gold. He found neither. Even though the islands were obviously already settled, Columbus continued to claim the lands for Spain and gave each place a Spanish name: Fernandina, Isabela, La Española (Little Spain), Santo Tómas.

By December, Columbus had been in the "Indies" for two months. Weather conditions were getting worse and in one storm the *Pinta* vanished. Heading north, the *Niña* and the *Santa Maria* found shelter from the strong winds and rain in the protection of an island Columbus named La Española (later called Hispaniola).

Exploring the island, Columbus became acquainted with the native Taino. Their chief, Guacanagari, liked Columbus and gave him gifts, including a mask with ears, tongue, and nose of hammered gold. When Columbus was ready to leave, Guacanagari and hundreds of natives stood on the shore and begged their visitors to stay, but Columbus was determined to find Cipangu.

The explorers were soon struck by very strong winds among dangerous rocks and reefs. After a day of stormy weather, the waters calmed and the winds died. On Christmas Eve the crew was too exhausted from the storm to do anything but collapse on the deck. Although Columbus had strictly forbidden the young boys of the crew to steer the ship, the tired helmsman turned the tiller over to one of the cabin boys and sank into sleep. As the boy gazed at the stars, the *Santa Maria* was gently carried by the current onto a reef. The boy cried out, and captain and crew tried desperately to keep the flagship from being lost on the rocks. The sail on the mainmast was lowered, ballast and cargo were thrown overboard, but the ship's hull was punctured by the rocks and water rushed into the *Santa Maria*. The men took the launches to the safety of the *Niña* and watched helplessly as the *Santa Maria* sank.

At dawn they rescued as much of the *Santa Maria*'s cargo and provisions as they could. A message was sent to Guacanagari telling him of the loss of the ship. Guacanagari immediately sent help and came to offer his sympathy. Over dinner, Columbus asked about gold and the Taino chief gave Columbus another gold mask, pointing to the nearby region he called Cibao. Columbus was reassured that there was gold in the area.

Since the *Niña* could not hold all of the men she and the *Santa Maria* had brought, Columbus decided to build a fort and leave some of the men on the island to look for gold. Many wanted to stay, and Columbus chose thirty-nine men. The Taino helped build the fort from the remains of the *Santa Maria*. Columbus named the fort La Navidad (Christmas Town) since it was built on Christmas Day. He left it stocked with food, trade goods, artillery, and seedlings for planting crops.

With only one ship, Columbus could no longer risk exploring. In the first week of 1493, he left the "Indies" and headed for Spain. The reliable trade winds that had pushed him westward to his goal were now blowing against him. Columbus correctly guessed that if he sailed north before heading east for Spain, he could avoid the trade winds.

The voyage had just begun when the *Pinta* was sighted and the two ships were reunited. Stopping at an island to make repairs, the explorers were met by natives. But these were not like the gentle people Columbus had found so far—the ships were greeted with a shower of arrows! Fighting back, the explorers wounded two men and the natives fled. Guacanagari had warned Columbus of the unfriendly Carib tribe known to eat human flesh. Columbus and his men quickly left the islands.

Soon they found themselves back in the Sargasso Sea being carried north by currents. A heavy winter storm forced the crews to bail seawater from the ships to keep them from capsizing. Although flares were kept alight to help the sailors of the two vessels keep each other in sight, on the second night of the storm the ships became separated. As the storm raged on, the men thought they would surely die. Praying for their souls, they promised to make a pilgrimage to a chapel if only God would spare their lives. Even Columbus did not think they would survive the storm. In desperation, he wrote the story of his voyage, sealed the letter in a wooden barrel, and threw it into the sea, hoping someone would find it and know of his great expedition.

The next day, the storm cleared and the weary men could see land. They had reached the Azore Islands, a Portuguese territory. Spain and Portugal were rivals for the possession of new lands and Columbus worried about an unfriendly reception. But his crew badly needed food, water, and rest. When they landed, several men went to give their promised thanks to God at the village chapel. The Portuguese governor had the men in the chapel seized, and only by showing a letter from the Spanish rulers could Columbus get his men released.

The ships once again faced stormy weather, now forcing them toward Portugal. The *Niña* was badly in need of repairs and Columbus sent Portugal's king a letter asking permission to land. King John summoned Columbus to his court and, hearing the story of Columbus's voyage, tried to claim rights to the lands Columbus had reached. Some of the court even suggested that King John murder Columbus, but he finally allowed Columbus to leave unharmed.

Columbus quickly sailed for Spain, where Martín Pinzón had already arrived with the *Pinta.* Though Pinzón had tried to tell the king and queen of the success of their journey to claim some of the glory for himself, the rulers had refused to see him until Columbus arrived. Pinzón returned home to Palos and died within a few days.

Columbus was received with great excitement. He had forced six Native Americans to come to Spain with him and had also brought a few parrots, a small sample of gold, and other items. As Columbus made the long journey to the Spanish palace, people crowded the roads to cheer him and touch the copper-colored natives he had brought with him.

At the palace, Columbus was received with honors. There was a grand procession and many festivities. Columbus told the king and queen that he had found the East Indies and that he had claimed the land there for Spain. The titles of Admiral of the Ocean Sea and governor of the islands he had found were solemnly bestowed upon him.

Columbus explained that a fort had been built so his men could stay and mine the gold that would make Spain a rich country. He proposed to return to settle the lands and bring back the gold. King Ferdinand and Queen Isabella were greatly pleased. Columbus had indeed proven himself.

The Second Voyage: 1493–1496

Both Christopher Columbus and the rulers of Spain were excited about the possibilities for trade and for making Christian converts in the "Indies." A large colony of three or four towns was planned near Hispaniola. Each town would have its own church for converting the Indians to the Catholic religion.

King Ferdinand and Queen Isabella had definite ideas for their new colony: they wanted the natives converted but felt they should be treated "well and honorably." They wanted Columbus to explore further to find "greater good things, riches, and more secrets." They also wanted Columbus to establish a trading business and promised him one-eighth of the profits. With little thought as to how these ideas would be accepted by the inhabitants of the "Indies," Isabella and Ferdinand sent Columbus back to Hispaniola.

Seventeen ships sailed across the Ocean Sea this time, including the stout *Niña,* which had been renamed the *Santa Clara.* Between twelve hundred and fifteen hundred men sailed with Columbus, and on this journey the ships also carried sheep, horses, and the provisions necessary to farm the land. Columbus sailed farther south on this voyage in the hopes of finding new islands. After an easy three-week voyage, land was sighted. Columbus named the island Guadaloupe and soon discovered it was inhabited by the cannibal Carib tribe. Most of the native men were away, so Columbus and his men safely explored the island. They found no gold and after a short stay sailed north.

As the ships approached La Navidad, the explorers saw little sign of life. Going ashore, they discovered two dead bodies. Their worst fears were confirmed as a search revealed the fort burned to the ground and every man dead. Columbus soon determined that his men had mistreated the natives and become greedy. The native people had defended themselves and there had been fighting.

Although the trust between the natives and Columbus's men had been broken, Columbus felt the mission of establishing a colony must go on. He found a suitable site near a native village and built a city he named Isabela. The Taino had told Columbus that gold could be found in the inland area of Cibao, so Columbus had Fort San Tomás built; there his men could mine the gold.

Neither the fort nor the city did well. The hot, humid weather and swarms of mosquitos made the men uncomfortable and they fell ill. The mining was slow and the farming difficult. In desperation, Columbus sent twelve ships back to Spain for food, clothing, medicine, mules, and more miners. He also sent a little gold, cinnamon, pepper, and twenty-six natives to be baptized.

The Taino were not pleased with the intrusion of the colonizers. The Europeans stole from them and the two groups quarreled. Although Columbus proved to be an unusually competent mariner, he was not a good governor. Unsure of what to do, he took three of the caravels and sixty men and went exploring, leaving his brother Diego in charge of the settlement and the problems.

Columbus still did not realize he was not in the Indies. He mistakenly believed that Cuba was mainland China. His men were tired, restless, and unsure whether Columbus had indeed found the East Indies or China. Columbus angrily threatened the men with physical punishment if they disagreed with him.

The stress of the expedition was showing on Columbus, who returned to Isabela so ill that he had to be carried ashore. Columbus was pleased to find that his brother Bartholomew had arrived at Isabela with three caravels of provisions from Spain, but many of the supplies Columbus had badly needed would not arrive until much later.

Life at the fort and Isabela was worse than when Columbus had left. The Taino were being used for slave labor in the mines. If they didn't produce a quota of gold dust they were severely punished. Thousands died from the poor treatment, overwork, and hunger. Others killed themselves rather than suffer. Attempts to convert the natives were unsuccessful, as the religion that worked for the Europeans made little sense to the natives whose culture was so different.

Columbus's men, disappointed with the hard work and slow progress, stole shamelessly and behaved horribly to the natives who had first greeted them as friends. Some of the settlers talked of mutiny and finally seized the ships Bartholomew had brought from Spain and sailed home.

Finally, Columbus decided he must return to Spain. His remaining ships had been destroyed in a hurricane, leaving only the tough little *Santa Clara*. Another ship was built from the wreckage of those destroyed and named the *India*.

Columbus could not control his men. In one final rampage, they seized hundreds of Taino and tortured and killed them. Thirty natives were taken as prisoners and packed onto the ships. The Taino were starving and cold on the return voyage, and those who didn't die were sold as slaves in Spain.

Columbus arrived in Spain discouraged and in poor health. He felt God must be punishing him, and for the rest of his life, he wore the plain, humble robe of the Franciscan monks.

Despite the mutineers' bad reports to the king and queen about Columbus, the monarchs spoke to Columbus of a return voyage. But Spain was at war with Italy, and Ferdinand and Isabella were arranging marriages for their children. It would be two years before Columbus would make another voyage to the colony of Hispaniola.

The Third Voyage: 1498–1500

During the two years that Columbus waited to return to Hispaniola, he heard rumors that a large landmass might exist west of Africa. He had also come to believe that precious stones and spices were most often found in the warm latitude countries. With these thoughts,

Columbus planned a new route to Hispaniola that took him farther south, across the equator.

Finding sailors was not an easy task now. More of the crews were criminals that Isabella and Ferdinand pardoned for sailing with Columbus. Six ships were prepared for the voyage, including the seaworthy *Santa Clara*. Among the crew was Bartolomé de las Casas, who would later actively oppose the mistreatment of the Native Americans.

Three ships sailed directly to Hispaniola while Columbus took the other three south to the Cape Verde Islands and then headed for the equator. Before they could reach the equator, the winds died and left them in a "scorching heat" that felt like "fiery furnaces." The ships sat motionless in the doldrums for eight days. The men feared the ships would catch fire and they would die.

When the wind picked up, the ships were taken west. It took seventeen days to find land. Columbus was now exploring the continent of South America. Finding the place where the Rio Grande and the Orinoco River enter the ocean, Columbus excitedly decided he had found the Garden of Eden. After staying long enough to gather pearls for the king and queen, Columbus sailed north for Hispaniola.

Columbus arrived at Santo Domingo to find a rebellion stirring. Francisco Roldán had led over one hundred men away. They demanded ships so they could return to Spain and Columbus was forced to provide them with two vessels. Columbus sent Ferdinand and Isabella a letter saying he had sent back unruly men and requested more religious replacements.

The king and queen realized that the colonies were in serious trouble. They heard many things about Columbus: that he was a good admiral but a poor governor, that he was a tyrant, and even that he was an enemy to Spain. They decided to send someone to investigate the situation for them. Francisco de Bobadilla was a royal officer they trusted. Giving him authority to act on their behalf, they sent Bobadilla to Santo Domingo.

Upon his arrival, Bobadilla could see that the colony's leadership had been poor. He had Columbus and his brothers, Diego and Bartholomew, put in chains and returned as prisoners to Spain. Columbus was a broken man. He refused to have his chains removed and continued to wear them even in Spain. The sight of the once-revered explorer dragging his chains was painful, especially for Columbus's sons Diego and Ferdinand. In despair, Columbus wrote a long letter to Isabella explaining his difficulties in Santo Domingo and the troubles he had suffered while trying to "uphold the rights of their highnesses." Columbus was brought to the court, where his humility and tears moved the king and queen to return his belongings. However, the monarchs had given Columbus's title of governor to a man named Ovando.

Meanwhile, on Santo Domingo, Bobadilla and the remaining three hundred men were committing shameless acts against the natives. Bartolomé de las Casas wrote, "The Christians should have loved and admired them but the Indians suffered and died in desperate silence . . . with not a soul in the world to turn to for help."

Columbus had begun his explorations with the hope of opening trade, bringing wealth to Spain, and bringing Christianity to the Indies. Nearly ten years later, his visions were shattered. He had not been able to find the wealth he expected. The lives of the Native Americans had been devastated, their freedom destroyed. Nearly fifty years old, Columbus was in poor health. Yet something within the explorer still sparked him to continue his mission and to try to regain his honor. Somehow Columbus convinced Isabella and Ferdinand to allow him one more voyage.

The Last Voyage: 1502–1504

By the time of Columbus's fourth voyage, explorers from many countries were traveling west across the Ocean Sea to the Americas. Columbus was given four caravels in rather poor condition for his last voyage. Although Ferdinand and Isabella had forbidden him to go to Hispaniola, he headed there. As Columbus approached, he saw signs that a hurricane was coming: long rolling waves, a heavy feeling in the air, an unusual tide, veiled clouds, and a red sunset. Even the seals and dolphins seemed to know it was coming and stayed near the surface of the water.

Columbus sent a message to Governor Ovando, warning him of the storm and requesting shelter in the harbor. With a fleet of over twenty ships about to leave, Ovando ignored the warning and refused Columbus's request. Columbus found shelter elsewhere, and the hurricane struck. All but one of Ovando's ships were lost in the fierce winds and pounding seas. Columbus and his men survived, though the ships were damaged.

Columbus continued to explore what is today Honduras, Nicaragua, Costa Rica, and Panama. He wanted to establish a fort but could not find a suitable harbor. The natives he found there dressed in fine clothing and wore swords and jewelry, but they were not particularly friendly and began preparing an attack. When several of his men were killed ashore, Columbus, exhausted and sick with malaria, fled with the remaining men, abandoning a ship.

Columbus headed for Santo Domingo for provisions and repairs before sailing back to Spain. When the ships were damaged during a storm, Columbus ran them aground. The marooned explorers lived in them for nearly a year before help arrived. Columbus confined his men to the ships to avoid trouble with the natives and asked the local Taino to provide food for the stranded men. After many months, Governor Ovando of Hispaniola sent enough ships for Columbus and the remaining men to return home.

Columbus returned to Spain for the last time. He was sick and had given up all hope. He could not feel good about his accomplishments—too many people had been hurt and none of the goals he had wanted to accomplish had been realized. Columbus felt betrayed and cried out, "May Heaven have mercy on me, may the earth cry for me, as I wait for death alone. . . . Hitherto I have wept for others; now . . . weep for me, whoever has charity, truth, and justice!"

Shortly after Columbus returned to Spain, Queen Isabella died. Ferdinand paid Columbus only a part of the money Spain owed the explorer and refused to return Columbus's titles to him. Columbus retired and kept a box of gold and the chains that once bound him near his bed. He even requested to be buried with the chains. In 1506, surrounded by his sons, brothers, and a few loyal friends, Columbus died. Few people even paid attention to the death of the explorer.

Bartolomé de las Casas wrote that Columbus was "the most outstanding sailor in the world, versed like no other in the art of navigation, for which divine Providence chose him." It is clear that Columbus accomplished many things. The sad events that followed the meeting of these two very different cultures may have been an inevitable outcome no matter who had landed in the Americas. Humans have had much to learn about each other. Today we can choose new ways to treat each other and be glad that our world has within it people of many colors, ideals, and visions.

Exploring Further

- Find out what Columbus learned from the Native Americans on his journeys. What did the Native Americans learn from Columbus? Make a list of what each group gained from the other.

- How might history have been different if Columbus had never gained support for his journey and had never sailed to the Americas? How else might the two cultures have come together? Would things have been different? Write a short story about what you imagine might have happened and share it with the class.

- Look for early maps of the world and compare them with today's maps. Find out what the symbols on a map mean. Determine the approximate miles Columbus traveled on each of his journeys across the Atlantic Ocean. List the journeys from shortest to longest.

- Research the Native American and the European views of land owner-ship. What kinds of problems did these different views cause as Euro-pean explorers claimed the Native Americans' lands for themselves? Write a paragraph stating your feel-ings about land ownership.

- In groups of two or four, draw one mural showing how the Native Americans might have viewed the meeting of the two cultures and one mural showing how the Europeans might have viewed the same meeting. Share the murals with each other. How do the murals differ?

- How would you feel if an explorer claimed your homeland for an-other country? Write an imaginary news release or make a cassette recording of a radio announcement about space visitors claiming Earth for another planet.

- Make a clay model of an early explorer's vessel, such as the caravels used by Columbus. Display it in the classroom.

- Listen to music that describes the sea (explore *La Mer* by Claude Debussy, *The Moldau* by Bedrich Smetana, *Sea Symphony* by Vaughan Williams, or environmental recordings of ocean sounds). Read about one of the storms Columbus sailed in. Write a paragraph or draw a picture describing the storm while you listen to the music.

- Research the different people who have "discovered" the Americas. Make a chart or time line of your findings.

- Read about the land, plants, and climate of Japan and China; then read about the Bahamas. Write a short paragraph or draw pictures describing them. Compare the two regions and write a paragraph pointing out how they are similar and how they are different.

Mary Kingsley
1862–1900

Overview

"Being human, Mary Kingsley must have been afraid of something, but one never found out what it was." English author Rudyard Kipling's words describe the unique Englishwoman who dared to enter territory that no European explorer had explored. Mary's desire to understand the culture, religious beliefs, and way of life of African people led her onto unknown and often dangerous paths. The information she gathered about them helped the world to understand the complex culture of the people in the vigorous African jungle.

Early Years

Born into Victorian society in 1860, Mary's unusual home life was instrumental in developing her fearlessness and strong curiosity. Her father, a doctor, was an adventurer at heart. George Kingsley traveled all over the world, using his profession as a means to explore other lands. His life was in danger more than once, and his family sometimes even wondered if he was alive.

George Kingsley was also an amateur anthropologist and brought home many artifacts from different countries. These were displayed in his study and were an endless source of wonder for Mary. The letters he sent home told of his interesting discoveries and exciting adventures, but he also wrote of the injustices native peoples suffered at the hands of European explorers and colonizers. His adventures were Mary's main connection to the outer world.

Mary's mother was her father's cook when they married. George's wife never traveled with her husband or became a part of his social world. When Mary was quite young, her mother became ill and remained in need of care for twenty-five years. Mary was a nurse to her mother and, when she was older, a research assistant to her father, as well as a housekeeper for her brother, Charles. Thus, the first thirty years of Mary's life were fully devoted to her family.

Although people viewed Mary as quiet and shy, her curiosity about how things worked was obvious even when she was a young child. She was somewhat mischievous, and her fascination for gunpowder and scientific experiments (she called them military engineering projects) often created havoc in the Kingsley household. She was just as likely to clean guns or dissect a frog as she was to sew or cook. She picked up her mother's cockney accent and some of her father's more colorful vocabulary as well as his delightful sense of humor. These traits often surprised people, coming as they did from a primly dressed Victorian woman.

Mary always felt she was poorly educated. As a woman of the Victorian period, she was not allowed the privilege of studying in schools and universities as her brother was. However, she learned to read, and reading became one of her favorite pastimes. From her father's library she read classics, books on mechanics, and accounts of explorers' expeditions. She taught herself chemistry, Latin, and physics. Mary's keen interest in Africa began when she read about Richard Burton, Paul Du Chaillu, Pierre Brazza, and David Livingstone and their nineteenth-century European explorations of Africa.

Mary had little opportunity to develop friendships as a child and young woman. At one point she wrote:

> *My life can be written in a very few lines. . . . It arises from my having no personal individuality of my own whatsoever. I have always lived in the lives of other people. . . . It never occurs to me that I have any right to do anything more than now and then sit and warm myself at the fire of real human beings. There is not one of them who has ever cared for me apart from my services.*

Toward the end of his life, George Kingsley retired and invited scientific people to teas in his home. Sitting and warming herself at their fire gave Mary new insight and ideas.

When Mary was thirty her father died. Within two months her mother died. In a way, this was when Mary was born. Their parents had left Charles and Mary with a modest amount of money and the family home. Mary's family obligations now only involved helping Charles to settle himself and then she was free to do as she pleased. She decided to take her first vacation. Following her father's example, she considered the more exciting and untouched foreign lands: South America and Africa. In the end, she chose to go to the Canary Islands, twelve miles off the coast of West Africa. Mary's first voyage from home lasted six weeks and provided her with a goal that she pursued for the rest of her life: to explore the land and understand the people of West Africa.

The Coast of West Africa: 1893

On Mary's vacation, her curiosity about the African continent was stimulated by the "Coasters" she met. These men traveled the West African coast and traded manufactured goods such as sugar, salt, calico, gunpowder, and fish hooks for the prized gold, silver, rubber, and ivory that were there in abundance. As agents for the West African trading firms, the Coasters had a great deal of direct contact and experience with the native Africans. Mary was enthralled by their stories. She was fascinated by the unfolding picture of these people whose lives were so different from her own.

When they first saw Mary, the Coasters thought she was from the Prohibition League and had come to check on their alcohol use, or that she was a missionary. The sight of a tall Victorian woman with bright yellow hair and deep blue eyes was unusual in West Africa. Mary wore black clothing after her parents died, often with a high-collared white blouse to accent the ankle-length, heavy black skirt, and a small bonnet and proper black shoes. She soon delighted the Coasters with her clever sense of humor, her direct nature, and her knowledge and interest in mechanics. Mary often said that she owed a great deal to the brave and determined Coasters who taught her how to live in Africa.

When Mary returned from her vacation, she knew that she would return to West Africa. Her goal appeared outlandish to the people of England. Women of her time traveled only to safe, comfortable vacation spots. Stories of life-threatening malaria and fever, cannibalistic tribes, and the dangers of wild animals made all but the very bold wary of going to West Africa. These fears were unfortunately confirmed by the few West African language books Mary could find to study. The simple phrases the books taught included such worrisome statements as: "Help, I am drowning!" "Why has this man not been buried? He was killed by a lion last week!" and "I am very sick."

Mary knew that her small income could not pay the expenses of her expedition. She immediately set out to find a way to fund her exploration. Newspaper editors and publishers did not believe she was able to explore Africa and offered her no support. But she discovered through research that not much was known about the fish in the rivers and off the coast of West Africa and decided she could do useful scientific work. Mary approached Dr. Gunther, who had written *A Study of Fishes* and worked for the well-known British Museum, and asked him to support her journey to collect West African fish specimens. If Dr. Gunther felt that her proposed journey was unusual, he kept his thoughts to himself. In fact, he was very excited at the prospect of the specimens she might bring back and agreed to ask the museum's board of directors for funding. Mary was delighted when the museum accepted her proposal and offered her more money than she would have dared to ask for. She immediately began preparations for her journey.

Explorers of Mary's time usually brought all of their provisions and survival equipment with them and traveled with a caravan of people. Sometimes they were carried in hammocks by Africans. Not only did Mary lack money to travel in this way, but she wanted to understand the native peoples and their customs and felt that she would raise less suspicion if she traveled as a trader and collector of scientific information. She later wrote, "When people see you want to buy or sell with them, they recognize there is something human and reasonable about you." Traveling as a trader also allowed her to be in contact with chiefs, witch doctors, and "that ever-powerful factor in all human societies, the old ladies."

Mary took only two bags with her: one medium-sized waterproof bag for blankets, boots, books, and her mother's .30 caliber pistol, and one bag of clothing. For her research she had a crate of specimen bottles and several gallons of pure alcohol to preserve the fish samples. She took her London clothing because "you have no right to go about in Africa in things you would be ashamed to be seen in at home." One of her greatest regrets was that she failed to bring enough hairpins and toothbrushes. The toothbrushes turned out to be a valuable trade item and she never seemed to have enough hairpins. When well-meaning friends urged her to take a respirator mask to avoid malaria, she replied, "Well! All I have got to say about that is that you need to be a better looking person than I am to wear a thing like that without causing panic."

In 1893, Mary left England for West Africa and traveled by boat to the Portuguese territorial town of Loanda. The ship had small cabins and smelled of dampness, copra (dried coconut meat), and palm oil. Its coal-fired steam engines edged it along at nine miles per hour. The temperature was usually around ninety degrees in Mary's cabin, even at midnight. It rained daily, pouring down in torrents, while at night lightning blazed and thunder roared. Mary was the only woman among the thirty passengers and the others soon discovered her to be a bold, curious, and enjoyable companion.

When Mary went ashore in Loanda, the officials were astounded by the presence of this unlikely woman explorer in her small, flowered bonnet. Her first journey from Loanda was to Calabar, a coastal town a thousand miles north. With a small group of African guides and helpers, she headed into the jungle with her bags, a tent, a few pots and pans, and her specimen jars. The expedition traveled mostly by dugout canoe. There were no seats, so they sat on the bottom of the canoe in two inches of dirty water.

Mary was enthusiastic about catching her first fish. The Africans found white grubs in rotten trees for bait and Mary began her scientific collecting by fishing from the leaky canoe amidst biting flies. Her first experience ended abruptly when one of the Africans accidentally hit another trying to avoid the sharp poisonous spikes of a catfish. The canoe overturned and left them all floundering in the river. Mary dried her clothing and Dr. Gunther's fish book by the campfire that evening. After that, Mary borrowed a canoe, learned to manage it, and often went fishing by herself. Mary was once approached by a hungry looking crocodile who placed its feet on the edge of her boat in an attempt to overturn it. To the amazement of the natives, she struck the crocodile with her paddle and quickly headed for shore.

Mary found she was often the first white woman the African tribes had ever seen. The people were generally astonished by her appearance, sometimes frightened. One group of creative African men walked her a mile into the jungle and sat her beneath a tree. Not knowing what they planned, she waited quietly but was relieved to discover that since she "was the queerest thing that they had ever seen" they had used her to draw curious monkeys down from the trees. When the creatures came down to examine her, the Africans promptly killed five of them and thanked her for her help.

The Englishwoman was cool, dignified, and unafraid. She would walk in front of her expedition as they entered an African village. Mary would find the chief's hut and ask for a place for her group to sleep. Surprised, the Africans would find a hut for her and feed her their food: palm oil stew, fried fish, snails, cassava or manioca, plantain, and pineapple. She graciously ate the food they served her but always provided her own tea.

After four months of traveling and collecting specimens along the West African coast, Mary returned home. Arriving in England, she admitted, "On my first voyage out, I did not know the Coast and the Coast did not know me, and we mutually terrified each other." During her trip to collect specimens, however, Mary had learned that she was strong enough to stand up to the heat, damp, and dangers of Africa—and she knew that she wanted to return.

Exploring the Interior of West Africa: 1895–1896

Delighted with Mary's success in collecting fish specimens, Dr. Gunther let her know the museum would support another such journey. The museum wanted not only samples of fish but insects as well. Mary was already preparing for a second trip, this time to explore the unknown interior of West Africa.

Although the English, French, Portuguese, and Dutch were all involved in trading with and colonizing Africa, no explorer had ventured up the two rivers into the interior of West Africa. In this region lived tribes whose way of life Mary felt was misunderstood by Europeans. She was particularly drawn to the spiritual and philosophical ideas of these people, their government and laws, and the structure of their lives. She also decided to do more serious trading as a way of connecting with the people and helping to pay for her journey.

Two days before Christmas in 1895 Mary left London, traveling as a companion to the wife of West Africa's British governor. Mary stayed in the government house at Calabar for a month, although she would have preferred to be on her way, sleeping in her tent in the African bush. She did, however, collect a number of specimens and planned her trip into the vast territory of the Ogawe River, where the Fan tribe resided. These fierce people were known for their cannibalistic habits, as well as for their intelligence.

Mary traveled by coastal steamer to the French port of Gabon, where the temperature regularly reached 110 degrees in the shade. From there she boarded a little stern-wheeler and headed up the Ogawe River to the Fan village of N'jole. On the way they made a stop at Lambarene, where Dr. Albert Schweitzer would later settle on his mission to heal Africa's sick and suffering people. At one of the Fan villages on the way to N'jole, Mary walked up a hillside to view the Ogawe River. In her proper London clothing, she slipped and rolled down the hill. She landed on the roof of a Fan hut and promptly fell through onto an old lady, a dog, and numerous cooking pots. The villagers thought the incident extremely funny, but the owner of the hut was angry. His loud shouting was silenced only after Mary gave him tobacco and the old lady a penknife. For years to come the villagers would talk about the day the white woman jumped through the roof of a hut.

Mary stayed for a while with a French missionary and his wife at N'jole. The villagers close to the coast were mostly friendly to white traders, though they were amazed by this peculiar white woman. Mary spent a great deal of time learning the language, customs, and spiritual beliefs of the Africans. She then wanted to travel upriver to gather fish specimens and explore the Fan villages that were mostly untouched by

European culture. The missionaries were greatly concerned about Mary's plan to go upriver. They warned her that Fans upriver would regard her much as she thought of her fish—as an interesting specimen! Even the local Fan villagers were wary of the more remote Fan tribes who were not accustomed to traders and were known for their ferocious customs. None of the local Fan villagers would go with Mary. Needing a guide and men to help her carry the specimen crates, she journeyed along the jungle paths to a village of the Igalwa tribe. These were a happy-go-lucky people who were good at handling canoes and were not cannibals. She found six Igalwa men to travel with her. Over the months they traveled together, Mary would come to know and appreciate her Igalwa friends. She gave them names of her own and learned about their native ways.

The Ogawe River was difficult to travel. In particularly treacherous stretches, Mary would leap from the canoe to shore, climb up the steep banks, and beat through brush to rejoin the canoe upriver.

At the first village upriver, the surprised Fans welcomed Mary but warned that the next three villages were not friendly and told her to avoid them. The explorers traveled cautiously at night to avoid being seen by the Fans in these villages. But the river was difficult and the explorers were too busy struggling with the rough water to be sure that they had passed all three villages. As they approached a village, one of the Igalwas named M'bo bravely went to find out where they were. To the explorer's great relief, M'bo returned to say they had found a friendly village.

The Fans had recently captured an elephant and were in an excellent mood to visit with Mary. They danced ceremonial dances while they pounded booming drums. Mary traded her collection of tobacco, fish hooks, beads, mirrors, and fishing line for ivory, rubber, and gold. At the next village, Mary welcomed the chance to rest in a hut, but twice during the night the village was stampeded by a frightened hippo. When scared, a hippopotamus runs in a straight line much like "a furniture van in hysterics" as Mary described it. After two stampedes and the destruction of a number of huts, she and the villagers gave up any attempt to sleep.

Earlier, the Fans in this village had caught a leopard and left the dangerous animal tied to stakes to starve. Feeling sorry for the animal, Mary pulled the stakes and let the leopard loose. The freed animal began to stalk Mary but quickly left when Mary said sharply, "Go home, you fool." A Fan watching from a distance was amazed at Mary's calm manner and the leopard's response. The story of Mary's strange power over wild animals soon spread.

As Mary prepared to go further upstream, three Fan warriors offered to travel with her and protect her. The Igalwas were becoming more nervous the further upstream they went and were glad to have the tough Fan warriors with them. For five days the explorers pulled the canoe upriver. Upon reaching the next village they had an uneasy feeling. Mary announced she would trade the next day, planning to barter briefly and leave quickly. But in the morning she discovered her three Fan guides had left to visit friends in a neighboring village. Afraid to leave without them, she bartered a full day and a half. She hoped the villagers would not realize they could kill her and take all of her trade goods for free.

When Mary had traded all of her goods she bartered her extra clothing, trading her stockings one at a time as head ornaments. She commented that her dozen blouses did not look particularly good "when worn by a brawny warrior wearing nothing else but red paint and a bunch of leopard tails." She had just bartered her final item—her toothbrush—when the missing Fans returned. Quickly, the crew gathered their belongings and headed downstream as fast as they could.

Two days later they reached the home village of the three Fan guides. The Fans advised Mary to go downriver as fast as possible, for word would spread quickly of the value of her trade goods. She could easily be killed for the rubber and ivory she now carried with her. Traveling by night the expedition paddled quietly past the three dangerous Fan villages, listening to the beating drums. They hid by sitting in the canoe out of sight during the day. Mary would never forget this experience and was relieved when they returned to N'jole on the fourth night.

No other explorer had dared to make the long, risky journey up the Ogawe River. Mary now had enough rubber and ivory to pay for her entire trip, and her jars were full of specimens she was sure had never been seen by European scientists. But in her mind, Mary Kingsley was already thinking of another journey.

Mary wanted to cross overland and explore her way back to the coast on the Rembwe River. She had heard stories of the gorillas that lived in the great silent forests between the Ogawe and Rembwe rivers. The overland trip meant walking a couple hundred miles through thick, dangerous jungle and alligator-infested swamps. Traveling by river had offered Mary protection from unfriendly tribes and animals, but the great forest would be an easy place to get lost in and was full of dangerous animals and deadly insects. Despite the dangers, Mary decided to make the journey and shipped her specimen jars down the Ogawe River to collect later.

The Adooma tribe traded regularly with the Fans and were on good terms with them. Mary chose four Adoomas to go with her and traveled by river toward the jungle. They had not gone far when a Fan warrior fired upon them from the shore. Mary angrily approached him and took his gun. The warrior explained that a man from a neighboring village had taken one of his wives. The warrior had fired upon Mary's group planning to kill one of them so they would feel obligated to help him get his wife back. Although this made no sense to Mary, she decided it was wisest to go with him to his village.

At the village a meeting was in progress. The villagers were so surprised by Mary's appearance that they offered to make her the commander in chief of a "war party" that was going to attack the neighboring village. She declined the honor but agreed to help the two tribes talk about the problem. She could speak a fair amount of the Fan language and could tell that neither village really wanted to fight. Somehow Mary settled the dispute without bloodshed and went quickly on her way.

When they arrived at M'fetta, the next village, a frightening Fan war party followed them along the river. Luckily, one of the Adoomas had a friend in M'fetta and was able to keep the war party at bay by calling for his friend. The nervous explorers waited twenty minutes while the villagers looked for the Adooma's friend Kiva. Mary later wrote, "I must say that never—even in a picture book—had I seen such a set of wild, wicked-looking savages as those we faced this night, and with whom it was touch-and-go for twenty of the longest minutes I have ever lived."

This village marked the end of their river travel. They began the long walk to the Rembwe River. Three M'fetta Fans, including Kiva, left the village with Mary. The Fans were strong and traveled very quickly. Luckily, they stopped every hour or so to eat, which allowed Mary and the Adoomas time to catch up.

Travel was difficult and they had to walk through dangerous swamps, climb over huge, rotting trees, and cross swiftly flowing rivers. In addition to these dangers, Mary fell into a pit dug to catch wild animals. It was only her ankle-length thick skirt that saved her from injury or death on the sharp ebony spikes planted in the bottom of the pit. In one village where they stopped to rest, Mary found a bag hanging on the wall containing various human body parts.

When they reached the village of Egaja, Mary's guides felt the village would not be friendly and prepared the guns they had brought. As Mary led the way into the Fan village, the natives stared at her in surprise. The incredulous chief agreed to let them stay in the village but asked Mary if she was a doctor. His wife had been bitten in the arm by a "fish like a snake" and was dying. Mary drained the badly abscessed arm and spent the night tending to a host of village injuries and diseases. In the morning Mary found the Fans had tied Kiva up and a man from a neighboring village was about to kill and eat him. The man said Kiva owed him trade goods and had not paid him back. Mary determined that Kiva did indeed owe the goods but managed to convince the villagers to let Kiva go by paying the angry Fan herself. She could see it was time to move on.

From the village of Egaja there was only one last great march. After four days' walk through thick forest, one of the guides found a band of gorillas. Quietly approaching within thirty feet of the magnificent animals, Mary watched them eating wild bananas and uprooting pineapples. Suddenly, a guide sneezed and the startled gorillas ran—luckily, in the opposite direction from Mary and her guide. Later, they came upon a band of gorillas on the overgrown forest trail. This time they were not so lucky. The male charged at Mary, and when he was fifteen feet away one of the Adoomas shot him with a hundred-year-old musket. Mary was greatly impressed by the ferocity of the animals.

The explorers had only one more swamp to cross. Carrying their loads high above their heads, the travelers waded through filthy water up to their necks. More than once Mary and her guides were submerged. Big brown leeches attached themselves hungrily to the explorers' hands and necks, making the people look as if they were wearing brown fur collars. After two hours they passed through the swamp and soon reached their destination, the fast-flowing Rembwe River.

At the trading village of N'dorko, Mary paid her companions with trade goods. She and the Adoomas were sad to say good-bye to each other, for they had become friends on their dangerous trek. The tribesmen returned to their village and Mary left downriver in a trading canoe. She arrived safely at the coastal trading village of Glass. The jungle drums had announced her arrival and the traders at Glass warmly greeted her.

Mary began her return trip to England. But on the voyage back she could not resist stopping at Mungo Mah Lobeh, the Throne of Thunder, today known as Mount Cameroon. She had been greatly impressed by the mountain and was determined to climb to its summit. Although climbers had reached the summit by a slow, westerly route, no one had yet attempted to climb the steep eastern side. Mary, of course, chose the difficult but shorter eastern route. With a group of local natives she climbed as high as 11,000 feet. In the extreme cold and snow, the natives could go no higher. Mary made camp for them and left by herself to climb the remaining 2,000 feet to the peak. There she left her calling card, then climbed back down the mountain.

When Mary reached England she was a national heroine. She modestly refused to give the press much information, but they gathered interesting stories from traders and Coasters. The tale of the quiet English girl who went off through the jungles with a pack of cannibals became exciting news throughout England.

Mary had became a well-known expert on West African ethnology. She prided herself on two things: her valuable contribution to European knowledge of West African people and natural history, and her ability to paddle a canoe as well as any Fan warrior. She was in great demand for giving lectures and writing magazine articles. She wrote two books about Africa and its people that became best-sellers. She also lifted her voice on behalf of the Africans. She was greatly concerned with the practices of the British colonial administration toward them. She promoted African self-rule and even spoke out against the well-meaning intentions of missionaries whose attempts to convert the Africans and change their customs were devastating to the native way of life.

But Mary missed Africa. She found it difficult to enjoy England fully. She wrote that living in West Africa "took all the color out of other kinds of living." At home, she surrounded herself with West African artifacts and kept her heat turned up to remind her of the West African climate. She missed being in the wilds. "My people are mangrove swamps, rivers, and the sea . . . it is a non-human world I belong to. The majesty and beauty of the [West African] scene fascinate me. I just lose all sense of human individuality, all memory of human life with its grief and worry and doubt, and become part of the atmosphere. If I have a heaven, that will be mine."

Why did the homebound Mary Kingsley become the brave explorer she did? She wrote in her book that she "went to West Africa to die . . . but it amused me and was kind to me and was scientifically interesting and did not want to kill me just then." But Mary did return to Africa to die. In 1898 a war began between England and the South African Boers, descendants of old-time Dutch settlers. Mary volunteered as a nurse and was placed in charge of one hundred prisoners. Within two months she contracted typhoid fever and died. She had requested that she be allowed to die alone and be buried at sea. Her request was honored and her coffin was dropped into the sea. Mary Kingsley would not leave West Africa again.

Exploring Further

- Find out what an anthropologist (such as Margaret Mead; Louis, Mary and Richard Leakey; or Gregory Bateson) does and make a presentation to your class.

- Visit a local museum and look at artifacts from other cultures. List five of these artifacts and describe what they were used for. What do they tell you about the society they are from?

- Draw pictures or cut photographs from magazines of ten things you feel are important artifacts of our present culture. Make a collage of the pictures and write a short description of these artifacts as if you were an explorer from another country who had never seen them before.

- Find out about another African explorer of the 1800s, such as Richard Burton, Paul Du Chaillu, David Livingstone, or Samuel Baker. Draw a picture illustrating one of his explorations.

- Mary traded goods for rubber and ivory on her journeys to West Africa. Find out more about ivory and whether it is still traded today. Write a short report about it.

- With a friend, make shadowboxes or draw a mural of what West Africa would have looked like during Mary's journeys in the 1890s. Compare this to Mary's London environment. Why do you think she preferred West Africa?

- Make clay models of three different kinds of fish species. Label your clay "specimens" with their scientific and common names and display them in the classroom.

- Explore the customs of the Adoomas, Fans, or Igalwas. With a friend, mime one of their daily activities and see if the class can guess what it is you are miming.

- Write a short story from the point of view of an African child seeing Mary, a white woman explorer, for the first time.

- Find examples of West African music, particularly mbira (kalimba), marimba, or kora music. Share them with the class.

- Find out about other women explorers, such as the wife of African explorer Samuel Baker, Alexandra David-Neel, Anne Lindbergh, Sally Ride, or Judith Resnick. Write a short report on one of their explorations. How are women becoming more involved in exploration?

- Find out what Albert Schweitzer and David Livingstone did in Africa. How did they help the Africans? Write a short report. What problems did European traders and colonists cause for the native Africans? How is this situation similar to that of the Native Americans? Share your thoughts with a friend.

Roald Amundsen

1872–1928

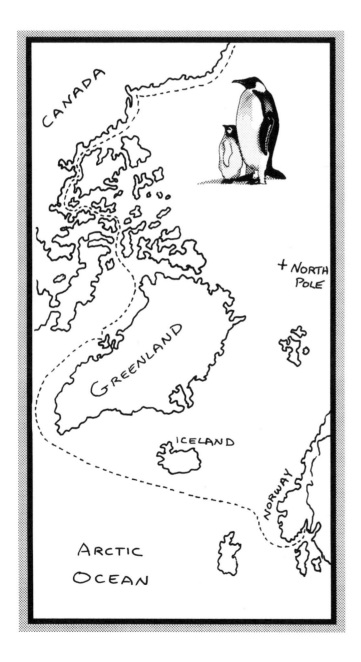

Overview

"How did I happen to become an explorer? It did not just happen, for my career has been a steady progress toward a definite goal since I was fifteen years of age. Whatever I have accomplished in exploration has been the result of lifelong planning, painstaking preparation, and the hardest kind of conscientious work." Thus Roald Amundsen described the sense of purpose that led him to become one of the world's greatest polar explorers.

Early Years

Amundsen came from a family of rugged Norwegian individualists who had grown up in the mountainous countryside around the Christiania Fjord. As a child, Roald learned to appreciate the contrasts of Norway's beauty and the intensity of the natural forces that surrounded him. His childhood prepared him in many ways for his later explorations into the harsh polar regions.

Jens Engebreth Amundsen, Roald's father, was a sailor, captain, trader, and shipwright. At the age of forty-three Jens married Hanna Sahlquist. He ran his home much like one of his ships, fairly but with strict discipline. He taught Roald a great deal about the sea and nature. Father and son had deep loyalty to one another and Jens's death at sea from illness was a great loss to fourteen-year-old Roald. Erik, a shipwright who had sailed for years under Jens, became one of Roald's friends and earliest teachers. There were no organized sports in Norway when Roald was a child, so the Amundsen boys devised their own physical activities. Gymnastics was becoming popular, and the boys rigged makeshift bars in a tree and soon became adept at gymnastic moves. Skiing was almost a national pastime, and Roald and his brothers had skis on as soon as they could walk.

When Amundsen was fifteen, he began reading the works of the great British explorer Sir John Franklin, whose explorations of the Arctic thrilled the young boy. Amundsen wrote that Franklin's

descriptions of the return from one of his expeditions thrilled me as nothing I had ever read before. He told how for three weeks he and his little band had battled with the ice and storms, with no food to eat except a few bones found at a deserted Indian camp, and how, before they finally returned to the outpost of civilization, they were reduced to eating their own boot leather to keep themselves alive. Strangely enough, the thing in Sir John's narrative that appealed to me most strongly was the sufferings he and his men endured. A strange ambition burned within me to endure those same sufferings. Perhaps the idealism of youth, which often takes a turn toward martyrdom, found its crusade in me in the form of arctic exploration.

Amundsen was so inspired by Franklin that he made the decision to become an arctic explorer. Amundsen kept his decision a secret, but he began to prepare for the hardships he knew he must endure. To be an explorer he needed a strong body. Roald participated in football, even though he did not like it, because it was the only organized sport available to him. He also went skiing as much as possible and wrote, "At every opportunity of freedom from school, from November to April, I went out in the open, exploring the hills and mountains which rise in every direction around Oslo, increasing my skill and hardening my muscles for the coming great adventure." He also insisted on sleeping with his bedroom windows wide open, even in the coldest weather.

Roald's mother hoped he would become a doctor, so he attended medical school, but he did not pass his first-year exams and never told her. When she died after his first year, he quit medical school and began to pursue his dream of becoming an explorer.

All Norwegian men were required to spend time in military service and Roald was excited about training. However, he was nearsighted, a condition he tried to hide so it wouldn't keep him from being accepted into the military. Fortunately, the doctor who gave entrance examinations was so amazed at Roald's physical development that he called in a group of coworkers to see Roald's impressive physical condition. In the excitement, the doctor forgot to check Roald's eyes.

Roald made many short excursions into remote areas of Norway. When he was twenty-two, he and a friend nearly died attempting to cross a plateau in winter that local people would not dare to cross then. The seventy-two-mile trip should have taken about a week. After the two men had been gone two weeks they were given up as lost. They had taken no tent or stove and had mysteriously lost their provision bag in a blizzard. During the journey, Roald was buried and frozen in the snow and his partner fell thirty-two feet over a cliff. Somehow, though, the two adventurers made it back to civilization, looking so haggard and gaunt that they were hardly recognizable.

Roald's reading had convinced him that an expedition leader must also be the captain of his exploration vessel. When leadership was shared between an expedition leader and a ship's captain, the crew's loyalties were often divided and disagreements would arise. So Roald set out to become a sea captain. He had learned much about the sea from the men in his father's shipbuilding company. To get his captain's license Roald worked on various arctic sealing ships and then signed on as crew with one of the great explorations to the Antarctic— an expedition led by Belgian Baron Adrien De Gerlache.

De Gerlache's scientific mission was to travel inland, survey the South Magnetic Pole, and map some of the uncharted areas of the Antarctic. The original plan was to leave a crew of four men, including Amundsen, in Antarctica through the winter and pick them up in the spring. The Belgian baron was determined to go farther south than anyone had ever gone before. His ship, *Belgica,* crossed the Antarctic Circle six months after leaving Europe. When winter approached and De Gerlache had not reached his southerly goal, he led the crew to believe they were heading home but instead took the *Belgica* farther south and deeper into the ice floes. Caught in storms, they were soon surrounded by ice and unable to escape for the winter. Now the entire crew was forced to become the first people to spend a winter in the Antarctic.

The expedition was not outfitted with enough winter provisions for the entire crew and the explorers found themselves in serious trouble. They did not have enough food, their clothing was not warm enough, and there were not enough lamps for the long nights. The men did not see the sun for several months, and then the red sun blazed continuously without any darkness. The fear that they would not survive hung over them like a dark cloud and two of the sailors went insane.

Amundsen and a Brooklyn doctor, Frederick Cook, were leaders in the efforts to survive the Antarctic hardships. They organized hunts to kill penguins and seals for fresh meat. De Gerlache was opposed to eating the meat, but when he and his crew fell ill with scurvy symptoms, Dr. Cook "prescribed" the meat as medicine and the men were revived. Only one crew member refused to eat the meat and died. For warmth, Amundsen found red wool blankets and made loose-fitting, warm clothing for the crew.

Dr. Cook persisted in searching for ways out of the ice pack. The crew felt his idea to cut a canal through the ice toward the main channel was a hopeless effort; however, they had little else to do. Using four-foot saws and explosives, they completed the difficult task in a few weeks. They had to wait a month at the edge of the channel before the pack ice broke up and allowed the *Belgica* to enter open water. For days the vessel moved slowly forward, squeezing between two giant icebergs as the nervous crew listened to the noises of ice grinding against the ship's hull. The sound was so loud that they could not hear anything else. But with the hull protected by penguin pelts that Dr. Cook had preserved and hung over the railing of the ship, the vessel moved through the ice and found open waters. The crew had survived the winter.

The vast amount of data the crew had recorded during their stay helped scientists to understand the climate of the Antarctic. The crew had also explored and mapped many uncharted areas. The intense two-year experience had taken its toll on twenty-six-year-old Amundsen, but the expedition had taught him a great deal about exploring. He now felt ready to lead his own expedition.

Navigating the Northwest Passage: 1903–1906

Looking for new trade routes had long occupied Europeans who desired valuable trade goods from distant lands. Hundreds of lives had been lost in almost sixty attempts to find a northerly passage between Greenland and Alaska. Forty rescue missions had been attempted to find the 128 men lost on the fatal Arctic expedition led by Roald's childhood hero, Sir John Franklin. The British explorer is credited with discovering the 900-mile Northwest Passage through channels between the islands of the Canadian Arctic in his 1845–47 expedition. However, no one had yet accomplished the mission of navigating the entire route. Roald Amundsen believed he would succeed.

Years earlier, seventeen-year-old Roald had stood among the welcoming crowds as explorer Fridtjof Nansen returned to his Norwegian homeland after having successfully crossed Greenland. As Roald later wrote, Nansen's return was

> a red letter day in many a Norwegian youngster's life. It was at any rate in mine. The young Norwegian skier sailed up the Christiania fjord on that calm and sunny day, his tall form glowing with the admiration of a whole world for the deed he had accomplished: "A madman's work"; the impossible! . . . With beating heart I walked that day among the banners and cheers and all the dreams of my boyhood woke to storming life. And for the first time I heard, in my secret thoughts, the whisper clear and insistent: If you could do the Northwest Passage!

For both Nansen and Amundsen, the Arctic world of cold and ice was an extension of their own familiar Norwegian environment. Nansen's innovative ideas broke new ground in many Arctic exploration techniques. He developed a lightweight sledge to pull supplies using the traditional Norwegian version as a model. He designed special clothing, tents, and even a cooking stove that conserved heat and fuel. Nansen also determined diet and calorie needs for working in extremely cold conditions.

Roald studied Nansen's techniques and thought carefully about the environment he would be exploring. Others had taken large vessels to battle the rough seas and dangerous ice. Amundsen's experience as a sailor in the Antarctic had taught him that a small vessel might allow him passage in places where large ships could not travel. From his experience in his father's shipyard he also knew that the shape of the vessel was sometimes more important than its size. Using his inheritance money, Roald bought the sixty-nine-foot sloop *Gjoa* (Yoo-ah).

Amundsen knew he must have a scientific purpose for his journey to get financial backing. The mysteries of polar magnetism were not yet completely unraveled. When Amundsen approached Geheimrath George von Neumayer with his proposal to discover the true location of the North Magnetic Pole, von Neumayer rose and said, "Young man, if you do that, you will be the benefactor of mankind for ages to come!" and offered his support.

But Roald needed a larger amount of money for the long journey and appealed to scientific societies and private patrons. When he was nearly ready to leave, one of his creditors demanded payment of his debts within twenty-four hours. The creditor threatened to take Amundsen's vessel and have him arrested for fraud if he did not pay. In desperation, Amundsen and his six companions boarded the *Gjoa* and quietly disappeared in the middle of the night, beginning the epic journey that would take three years to complete. "The great adventure for which my whole life had been a preparation was under way!" exclaimed Amundsen. The ship was loaded above and below decks with crates of provisions and equipment. The seventeen fierce Eskimo dogs they had brought for overland explorations strained at their tethers and barked continuously.

Despite freezing fog, gales, and icebergs, the seven explorers successfully made the perilous journey to the heart of the Canadian Arctic and dropped anchor. Here they began their magnetic observations. Scottish explorer Sir James Ross had located the North Magnetic Pole in 1831, but scientists had a theory that the magnetic pole shifted locations. Amundsen set out to confirm the nature of the magnetic pole through scientific measurements. To do so he would have to navigate closer to the pole through dangerous waters. Because of magnetic interference, the valuable magnetic compass would be useless. The crew knew they risked their lives traveling without the aid of the compass, and the men stood nervous six-hour watches each night as they sailed cautiously through the fog.

Their worst fears were realized when the *Gjoa* suddenly grounded on a large reef. The eight-foot draft of the vessel was too deep for the shallow reef that extended for two hundred feet in front of them. When high tide failed to lift them off the rocks, Amundsen ordered twenty-five of the 100-pound cases of dried rations thrown overboard to lighten the load. Gale winds rose and the crew raised the ship's sails in hopes that the gusts would blow the ship off the reef. The *Gjoa* began moving. Then the crew sighted foaming water over protruding rocks near the end of the reef. Amundsen ordered the crew to abandon ship, fearing the vessel would break up on the rocks. But at the desperate suggestion of a crew member, the remaining deck cargo and some of the crates from the hold were heaved overboard instead. The *Gjoa*, after being lifted up by the sea and pounded onto the rocks several times, finally reached the end of the reef.

The storm worsened, and the drenched and exhausted crew had no rest till the gale left them at Boothia Peninsula. Now the danger was the rapid approach of winter, and their survival depended on finding a safe haven. They located an ideal position on King Wilhelm Island only ninety miles from where Sir James Ross had located the North Magnetic Pole. The explorers settled in for the winter and built several wooden buildings: observatories, a storehouse, a firehouse, and dog kennels. They used copper nails and marble slabs that did not interfere with the magnetic signals of their observation equipment.

Soon the explorers were discovered by the native people, the Eskimos. The Eskimos' elders had told them of the *kabluna* (white man) encountered seventy-two years earlier, referring to the Ross expedition. The Eskimos were surprised and delighted by Amundsen's arrival. When Amundsen invited the Eskimo people to visit his camp, two hundred men, women, children, and dogs appeared. They set up nearly fifty ice huts by the *Gjoa*, which was now frozen in the winter ice.

Amundsen was delighted to have the chance to find out how these people lived. Many polar explorers with sophisticated equipment had died in the harsh Arctic while these native people lived in simple harmony with the land. He learned invaluable skills from his Eskimo friends. When the explorers visited the large Eskimo village, they attempted to build their own sleeping igloos. The Eskimos laughed at the Norwegians' awkward attempts and Amundsen was forced to ask his giggling hosts for help.

The Eskimos gave gifts of fur clothing to the crew, and the men quickly discarded their wool clothing. The native people also taught the men a great deal about traveling in the frozen lands, especially how to handle the Husky dogs. This lesson would later be one of the most significant factors in Amundsen's success in reaching the South Pole.

The nineteen months that Amundsen spent in the Canadian Arctic islands provided enormous quantities of scientific data. The magnetic observations were so complete that it took scientists nearly twenty years to analyze the information fully. Of equal importance were the surveys and charts Amundsen and his crew made of one of the last unknown stretches of North America. Amundsen also returned with a collection of Eskimo artifacts that he donated to Norwegian museums.

The crew spent two long winters in the icy Arctic and when open water appeared beyond the tiny bay that harbored the *Gjoa,* hopes for escape ran high. Weeks passed without a break in the ice between the *Gjoa* and the open water, but finally the *Gjoa* was able to sail free. The Norwegians took with them a seventeen-year-old Eskimo named Manni, who pleaded with Amundsen to be taken along.

The expedition sailed west through hazardous and uncharted waters. When the ship reached the entrance to the straits between Victoria Island and the mainland, Amundsen knew he had been successful, for other explorers had reached the same point from the opposite direction. The Amundsen expedition had completely navigated the long, difficult Northwest Passage.

The explorer's excitement soon cooled when the *Gjoa* was locked by ice in Alaska's Mackenzie Bay. The men now faced another Arctic winter. This time, six American whaling ships were also stuck in the ice and would at least be company. Determined to tell the world of his success, Amundsen set off for the closest telegraph office—a 500-mile journey over 9,000-foot-high mountains through deep snow.

The trip was supplied by a captain of one of the whaling ships, a sixty-year-old seafarer named Mogg. Overweight and in poor condition, the captain rode in a sledge while Amundsen and two Eskimo guides ran alongside. They covered twenty-five to thirty miles a day. Mogg had refused Amundsen's suggestion to take pemmican (a mixture of dried meat and fat) and instead brought cooked and frozen beans. Mogg ordered the runners to skip lunch so as not to waste time. With reduced rations of only beans, the runners became dangerously thin and hungry. Always aware of physical needs, Amundsen threatened to leave the plump captain in the wilderness unless he allowed adequate rations. Scared at the thought of trying to survive alone, Mogg quickly agreed.

Forty-two days from the start of their overland journey, Amundsen and his companions reached what is now Eagle City and telegraphed the exciting news of Amundsen's success to the world. He waited in the Arctic outpost two months for letters to his crew to arrive, then made the five-week journey back to his ship. When he reached the *Gjoa,* he found that his engineer, Gustav Wiik, had died of appendicitis. Another disaster struck during their wait for the ice to break up when Manni fell into the icy water. Like most Eskimos, Manni did not know how to swim, and he quickly disappeared in the freezing water.

When the ice broke, the *Gjoa* headed for Nome. Having navigated 3,450 miles of Arctic waters, the Norwegians were surrounded by welcoming boats upon their arrival. The ship then sailed south and the crew presented the *Gjoa* as a gift to the city of San Francisco, where it still stands in Golden Gate Park.

Amundsen's first expedition had been undeniably successful. He lectured in the United States and Europe during 1906–1907 and returned to Norway a hero with enough funds to repay all his creditors. More than that, he had gained invaluable knowledge of polar exploration and the dream of another expedition: to be the first to reach the true North Pole.

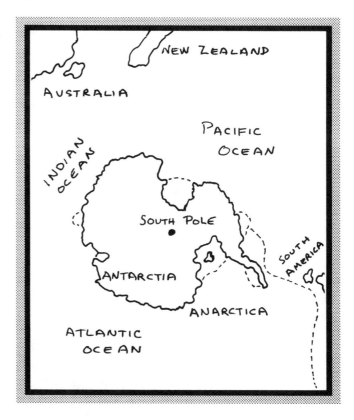

The Expedition to the South Pole: 1910–1912

A race to become the first to reach the North and South poles began among polar explorers. When Amundsen returned to Norway from the Northwest Passage, he immediately began preparing for an expedition to the true North Pole. He also wanted to confirm Fridtjof Nansen's theory that a ship drifting with the ice pack would drift across the Arctic pole. Roald spent two years planning the expedition and preparing the *Fram,* the 119-foot ship he had borrowed from Nansen. But in 1909 newspaper headlines proclaimed that the North Pole had been reached by none other than Amundsen's fellow crew member on the De Gerlache expedition, Dr. Frederick Cook. One week later, the papers carried the claim that American Admiral Robert Peary had also reached the North Pole. A dispute raged that was eventually settled when Peary was declared first and Dr. Cook was declared a fraud.

Dr. Cook discouraged Amundsen from continuing his plans to reach the North Pole. Even though a test of Nansen's drifting theory would be valuable and had not been either Cook's or Peary's method of reaching the pole, the race to the North Pole had ended. But no one had yet reached the South Pole, though an explorer named Ernest Shackleton had come close.

A few days after Amundsen decided to attempt such an expedition, English navy captain Robert Falcon Scott announced his plans to locate the South Pole. Amundsen kept his plans a secret and completed his preparations as if still heading for the North Pole. In 1910 he and his crew took ninety-seven Greenland Huskies aboard the *Fram* and left at midnight.

Amundsen supposedly planned to sail around the southern tip of South America and up to Alaska to begin the Arctic drift. When the *Fram* reached the Madeira Islands, however, Amundsen explained his plan to find the South Pole to the crew and asked each man if he wanted to continue on the expedition. Roald's brother Leon took letters from each of the men to their families and announced Amundsen's new destination to the world. He also notified Scott of the news and the race to the South Pole was on.

Amundsen and his crew sailed sixteen thousand miles to reach the Ross Ice Shelf, then called the Great Barrier. A massive floating shelf of ice formed by glaciers pouring down from the mountains in the interior of Antarctica, the shelf is nearly the size of Texas. Giant pieces were known to break off and become floating, flat-topped icebergs. Though it had never been attempted before, Amundsen decided to set up a base camp on the ice shelf, which he named Framheim. This base placed his expedition sixty-nine miles closer to the pole than his rival Scott's base at McMurdo Sound.

Scott planned to travel to the pole using tractorlike motorized sledges and Manchurian ponies, but Amundsen held to his belief that dogs and lightweight sledges were most practical for polar travel. He redesigned the sledges to reduce their weight from 165 pounds to 48 pounds each. His men wore lightweight versions of the practical fur clothing the Arctic Eskimos had given him.

Amundsen planned every aspect of the journey for quick but safe travel. His plan called for depositing over three tons of provisions at specific locations along the route to the South Pole. The depots would allow the team to travel lightly in their final burst for the pole. For food, Amundsen used mostly pemmican, to which he added oatmeal and peas to improve digestion. Snow beacons and pennants were staked in the snow for miles on either side of the depots to ensure that they could be found again. The explorers would continue to deposit food as they headed toward the pole, lightening their load on the way and providing enough supplies for their return journey. Even though Amundsen loved animals, he determined the points where the Huskies would no longer be useful and could be killed to provide food for both the men and the remaining dogs. After establishing the first three supply depots, the team returned to the ship for more provisions and prepared for the final trek.

Nervous about losing the race to the pole, Amundsen began the final journey too soon. The temperature plummeted to -69 degrees and two men were frostbitten. The party was forced to return to the base camp. More than a month later the five men making the journey to the pole were able to resume their mission safely.

Scott's expedition started twelve days after Amundsen's. He had also established supply depots at specific points along his route. But the Manchurian ponies did not do well in the harsh cold. They floundered in the deep snow and the snow machines did little better. Unlike Amundsen, Scott conducted scientific research on his way to the pole and even carried thirty pounds of rocks to the end. Scott's journey proved a difficult trek.

Amundsen's route had never been traveled before and was later said to have been the most difficult he could have chosen. His path led the explorers through crevasse fields where the men struggled across deep gaps, sometimes having to rescue dogs, sledges, and even each other from the cracks that had been covered by snow.

Amundsen soon reached another obstacle: a glittering mountain range with a glacial river of ice flowing from it. Day after day, the expedition inched past deep chasms and around towering blocks of ice. Blizzards and gale-force winds stopped the Amundsen team, and when they began again, they soon found their path led through what they named Devil's Glacier. At times they had to scale hundred-foot ice ridges. The crystallized snow felt like sand blowing in the wind.

Amundsen's final depot was built just past the southernmost point reached by Ernest Shackleton's expedition two years earlier. Amundsen's team was now moving farther south than any other human had ever been. Unfurling the Norwegian flag to commemorate this spot, Amundsen could not hold back his tears of joy at the accomplishment. With a month's supply of food, the men headed for the pole enjoying perfect weather. A week later they were within a day of the South Pole. Amundsen awoke throughout the night with "the same feeling that I can remember as a little boy of the night before Christmas Eve—an intense expectation of what was going to happen." The next day they reached the South Pole and were at the bottom of the world.

There was nothing to distinguish the South Pole by looking at it—only endless snow and ice. The men measured their position by the sun every hour for twenty-four hours to ensure they were at the right place. When they had done so, Amundsen and his companions planted the Norwegian flag at the South Pole. To avoid any question that their expedition had indeed reached the pole, they planted additional flags every six miles in three directions.

The men stayed at the South Pole three days. Continued good weather made the return journey easy. Despite losing sight of their landmark in a blizzard once, they arrived at Framheim on January 26, 1912. The expedition had traveled 1,860 miles in ninety-nine days. The men celebrated with champagne; the cook had kept it from freezing by sleeping with it all winter.

Amundsen began his return home, but in New Zealand he and the crew heard the devastating news: Scott and his exploration team had reached the South Pole but had died of cold and starvation on their return journey. Their provisions had been too few, too small, and too far apart. Amundsen was crushed by the deaths.

Scott became a British hero, and Amundsen was accused of forcing Scott to make poor decisions by creating a race for the pole. But Amundsen told reporters, "I would gladly forego any honor or money if thereby I could have saved Scott his terrible death." In spite of the tragedy, Amundsen's journey to the South Pole has been called a "work of art" and remains one of the greatest examples of planning an expedition in the history of polar exploration.

The Polar Explorations by Air: 1925–1926

For his next expeditions, the Norwegian explorer had a new ship built that was shaped very much like an egg cut lengthwise. The vessel's bottom was rounded so that if she were caught in grinding ice, the pressure would lift her up rather than crush her. Amundsen christened his ship the *Maud* in honor of Norway's queen.

In 1918 Amundsen left Norway to navigate the Northeast Passage from Norway to Alaska along the Arctic coast of Russia. The five-year journey would prove to be an ordeal; Amundsen narrowly escaped being mauled by a polar bear and fractured his right shoulder. With no doctor aboard, it was not properly set. He was unable to lift his arm, but was determined to cure himself. He exercised daily until he could use his arm freely again. Later, x-rays of his shoulder proved that his recovery was miraculous.

Amundsen also suffered from serious carbon monoxide poisoning that left him ill for days and caused heart trouble that plagued him for years. For many months he could walk only short distances without becoming tired. Doctors advised him that he could no longer safely withstand the physical exertion of exploration, but Amundsen refused to accept their conclusions. Nine months later he successfully made one of the hardest physical treks of his life, traveling fifty miles a day through snow and ice.

Scientists and geographers still did not know whether the Arctic Ocean contained a land mass or was only ice and water. In 1925 the fifty-two-year-old Amundsen began making plans to find out. This time his expedition would be by air. He placed his finances in the hands of a business manager who promised to raise enough money to buy a seaplane for the expedition. The business manager, however, was a fraud and left Amundsen penniless. Amundsen's angry creditors included his brother Leon, who sued Roald for money he had borrowed for earlier expeditions.

One of Roald's favorite sayings was "When it is darkest there is always light ahead." The light came to him in the form of Lincoln Ellsworth. An aspiring American explorer with a wealthy father, Ellsworth greatly admired Amundsen. Ellsworth's father reluctantly gave the explorer the eighty-five thousand dollars needed to purchase two seaplanes. Together Ellsworth and Amundsen planned a 1,700-mile flight over the Arctic Ocean. The seaplanes were carried aboard two ships through 580 miles of rough seas and storms to a Norwegian mining community only 750 miles from the North Pole.

Flying at seventy-five miles per hour, the expedition leaders and four crewmen covered a distance that would have taken weeks by dog sledge. Amundsen had to calculate their location by dead reckoning. After eight hours, he believed they were over the North Pole, but to know for sure they would have to land.

The pilots searched for a large enough stretch of water among the twisting leads and broad expanses of ice covered with mounds and ridges. Finally they saw a large patch of open water. But as they approached, the site appeared too narrow for safe landing. One plane, leaking fuel because it had lost rivets during takeoff, suddenly developed engine trouble and was forced to land in the narrow channel. It brushed the top of an iceberg on its descent and stopped with its nose pressed against a rising sheet of ice. The other plane found a better landing location ten minutes away, but the seaplane stopped so gradually that it hit a giant ice floe and began to fill with water. The engine had been jammed during landing and would not run. The men were now separated, their planes were damaged and had less fuel than expected, and they had a limited amount of food.

Measurements showed they had drifted west, missing the pole by 156 miles. They were nearly 600 miles from civilization. The two crews were not even sure how to find one another. After two days, they spotted each other by climbing ice ridges and searching with binoculars. When the drifting ice floe brought the planes within two miles of each other the men were able to communicate using flag signals. Since each signal had to be looked up in an instruction manual, the tedious communication took several hours. The conversation revealed that Ellsworth's plane could not be repaired, but luckily Amundsen's could fly.

When the crews had drifted to within half a mile of each other, Ellsworth and his partners set out for Amundsen's group. Traveling on the shifty ice was dangerous and they had to move in a roundabout way to avoid open expanses of water. All but Ellsworth fell through the thin ice into the water, and one of the crew nearly drowned before the three shivering men finally reached Amundsen and his crew.

The explorers knew they were in a race against death by starvation. Their choices were limited. The seaplanes could take off on water or smooth ice. They had neither. A walk to civilization was probably a hopeless journey. They could try to build a smooth runway and attempt to take off or they could haul the plane to open water.

After several unsuccessful take-off attempts, the desperate men found a flat stretch of ice about half a mile away and laboriously chopped a channel to move the plane. A week of shoveling and tamping snow on the ice created a smooth runway. Amundsen guessed they moved three tons of ice during their long ordeal. The plane was constantly being frozen into the water and the crews had to chop it out to keep the ice pressure from crushing it. Tempers flared and "polar nerves" set in, making little annoyances seem like monumental disturbances.

With time running out, the crew unloaded everything from the plane, and the six men crammed into it. They would not have many chances to take off. After one disappointing attempt, the dangerously overloaded seaplane finally rose into the air. Now the crew had to find their way back. With only a magnetic compass that did them little good so close to the magnetic pole, they were flying blindly. Fog made the journey even more difficult and they watched the fuel gauge drop as they flew south. Eight hours later they recognized an Arctic island and shouted for joy just as their equipment failed. They had to land immediately. They quickly found a patch of clear water and landed the plane successfully.

A dangerous journey to civilization still lay before the crew. As they became aware of the horrifying prospect they sighted the sail of a sealing ship, and with their last bit of fuel, bounced their seaplane across the water toward the ship and rescue. The sealers did not recognize the bearded and sunburnt crew. When Amundsen pointed out his famous eaglelike profile, the sealers greeted them with enthusiasm. The explorers learned they had been given up as lost and Ellsworth's father had died while they had been gone. The expedition's supporter would never know his son had been successful.

The crew returned with important scientific information about ice drift and climate conditions near the North Pole. They also confirmed that no land existed on the European side of the Arctic. Amundsen and Ellsworth were greeted as heroes. The two explorers were undaunted by their brush with death. They had each found a reliable and compatible companion, and they began plans for another attempt to fly across the Arctic—this time in a dirigible.

Ellsworth put up one hundred thousand dollars to buy a dirigible from the Italian Army. The contract required, however, that the Italian dirigible designer, Colonel Umberto Nobile, be hired as pilot, share the command, and have his name included in the expedition title. Not pleased with this arrangement, Amundsen and Ellsworth refused to put Nobile's name in the expedition title. Throughout the trip, Nobile would seek personal glory and argue with the expedition leaders.

A hangar was built in King's Bay to house the huge dirigible, now named the *Norge* (for Norway), as preparations were made to cross the Arctic Ocean. Again, a race was on. Richard Byrd was mounting his own expedition over the pole by airplane. Two days before the *Norge* would leave, Byrd conquered the North Pole by air in a fifteen-hour flight. The validity of Byrd's flight is to this day contested, however. Amundsen and Ellsworth continued their plans.

The *Norge* crew consisted of the two explorers, fourteen crewmen, and Nobile's dog. The greatest danger to the expedition was the weather; many problems could arise if ice formed on the dirigible. Because it used highly explosive hydrogen gas, no cooking or heat was allowed; the temperature aboard was so cold the sandwiches froze.

The order was given to loosen the ropes that held the dirigible to the ground and she rose slowly on her epic ascent. Fifteen hours after they took off the explorers sent a radio message saying they had reached the North Pole. Amundsen and his friend Wisting, who had made the South Pole expedition, had become the first men to visit both poles. Wisting, Amundsen, and Ellsworth ceremoniously dropped Norwegian and American flags attached to steel-tipped poles to the ground. True to Nobile's display of grandeur on the journey, he dropped an armful of Italian banners and an Italian flag so large it temporarily hung up on one of the engines and threatened to tangle in one of the propellers.

The *Norge* circled the pole for an hour then set a course for the other side of the world. But two hours later it was surrounded by fog. With poor visibility the crew had to navigate by radio signals. The fog began condensing into ice that tore the dirigible's delicate canvas covering. The ice could pierce the gas containers and cause a loss of hydrogen fuel. Ice coated the radio aerial and the radio stopped working. Unable to navigate by radio waves, Ellsworth and Amundsen found themselves at the mercy of the unreliable magnetic compass.

The world had lost contact with the explorers and for two days waited anxiously while bad weather engulfed the delicate dirigible. When the weather cleared enough for the crew to use a sextant to determine their location they found themselves only twenty-one miles west of their planned route. They could see land, but finding a landing site proved difficult. Fog, storms, and ice continued to plague them. At times the *Norge* rose high into the air, and then dropped dangerously close to the ground. Nobile proved to be lacking in piloting abilities, and more than once Amundsen's pilot took over and saved the expedition. Still short of its destination, the dirigible made a forced landing with an improvised anchor over an unidentified village. The anchor hit the ground, but the *Norge* dragged dangerously in the wind, threatening a fiery crash. Finally she stopped and began to release hydrogen. It had been seventy hours and forty minutes since departure. The explorers had traveled 3,390 miles at an average speed of forty-five miles per hour.

The Amundsen-Ellsworth expedition had crossed over the North Pole and seen the top of Earth from the air. The world greeted them as heroes. In Norway, Ellsworth was honored as a foster son and called a "modern Viking," and the Norwegians named a mountain after him. Both Amundsen and Ellsworth received medals of honor.

Nobile sought his own glory arriving in Seattle in a glittering uniform. A serious split arose between Nobile and the two commanders as Nobile took personal credit for the mission and denounced the other commanders and crew. Amundsen angrily responded to the accusations.

Now in his early fifties, Amundsen retired. He had become one of the great polar explorers and was often called "The Last Viking." Nobile, however, purchased another dirigible, the *Italia,* and returned to the Arctic to survey coastal areas off Siberia, Canada, and Greenland.

Nobile's poor piloting skills resulted in the crash of the *Italia* on her return trip from the pole. Six crewmen were killed in the crash, and Nobile and nine others were left on the ice. When the world lost radio contact with them, several rescue missions began. Fifty-four-year-old Amundsen, who greatly disliked Nobile, announced that he would join in the search.

The French government gave Amundsen a newly designed seaplane that he suspected was unsuited for the arctic. It was also overloaded. But on the same date the explorer had set out years ago to conquer the Northwest Passage, he left on his rescue mission. Meanwhile, Nobile had managed to repair his radio and had transmitted his location. Though it was clear that there was no hurry for the rescue, Amundsen continued with a thirty-hour supply of fuel. Two days passed. The world began to wonder where Amundsen was, but the victorious Norseman had always survived. The focus remained on rescuing Nobile as several countries sent missions.

Amundsen's birthday passed and was a day of sadness and worry. Six ships were now hunting for the famous Norwegian explorer. Ten weeks after his disappearance, pieces of a seaplane were found by a fishing boat and identified as the type of seaplane Amundsen had been flying. The pieces appeared to have been used as a makeshift life raft. Amundsen and his crew died while the international rescue mission for Nobile was completed.

Though Amundsen was presumed dead, many Norwegians refused to believe that he would never return. A reporter remembered the words Amundsen used to recount his love of the Arctic: "If you only knew how splendid it is up there! That's where I want to die; and I only hope death will come to me chivalrously, that it will overtake me in the fulfillment of a high mission, quickly, without suffering." The last great Viking now rested in the land that had fascinated him since he was a child.

Exploring Further

- Plan your own expedition to one of the poles. Make a list of things you would take on your journey.

- Research and compare the Arctic and Antarctic. Make a chart of the similarities and differences between the polar ecosystems.

- Find photographs or drawings of polar landscapes. Using white chalk on blue paper, or white and blue oil pastels, draw a picture that communicates your vision of the icy world.

- Research the difference between the true pole and the magnetic pole. Write a short report about polar magnetism and share it with the class.

- Find out about the Northern Lights and write a poem that describes them.

- The International Geophysical Year included a worldwide effort to research the Antarctic. Make a list of some of the IGY activities and accomplishments.

- Make a time line showing the dates of various explorers' expeditions in search of the Northwest Passage.

- Find out how long the longest Arctic days and nights are. Write a short story about living for long times in total light or total darkness.

- Make a mind map showing Amundsen's accomplishments, including his findings in ethnology and natural history.

- How did Amundsen's relationship with the Eskimos compare with the relationships of Columbus or Mary Kingsley with the native peoples they encountered? Write a short report about your feelings.

- Explore the customs of Eskimo people. Make a list of things they shared with Amundsen that helped him in his later explorations.

Jacques-Yves Cousteau
1910–

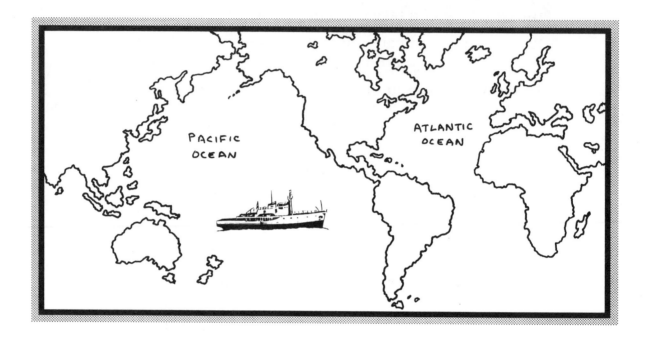

Early Years

Daniel Cousteau was a busy French lawyer working for an American millionaire when his wife, Elizabeth, gave birth to their second son. They named him Jacques-Yves Cousteau. Although the Cousteau family lived in France, Daniel's work took him and his family to many places around the world. One of Jacques's earliest memories is of being rocked to sleep on a train.

Young Jacques was a curious child who read many books, especially books about the sea. His family spent summers by the sea in France. Jacques loved to play and swim in the Atlantic Ocean. He liked to watch ships float on it and see stones sink in it. This wonderful feeling for the ocean would stay with him all his life. Someday he would know more about the undersea world than anyone else on Earth.

When Daniel's work took him to New York City for a year, the whole family moved with him. Jacques was ten and "Jack," as his friends called him, learned to speak English well but with a heavy French accent.

During his summer in the United States, Jacques went to summer camp in Vermont. One of the counselors asked him to remove branches caught beneath the diving board at the lake. Jacques was a good swimmer and worked very hard, diving as deep as twelve feet in the murky water without goggles or a mask.

Remembering a story he had read about a hero who hid underwater from villains and breathed through a hollow reed, Jacques decided to see if this would work. Putting a garden hose through a piece of cork, he left one end of the hose above the water, took the other end in his mouth, and tried to breathe. It didn't work, but he remained curious about finding a way to breathe underwater. This fascination was later to guide him to explore, work, and even live beneath the ocean.

Jacques also enjoyed finding out how machines worked and designing new ones. When he was eleven, he used the blueprints for a two-hundred-ton floating crane to build a four-foot electric-powered model. But he also added some new design features. When engineers saw his additions, they were astounded and later used his new ideas to improve their cranes. When he was thirteen, Jacques built an electric car.

Jacques saved his allowance and bought one of the first movie cameras ever sold in France. He immediately took it apart and put it back together to see how it worked. He loved to make his own movies. He always gave himself credit at the end of his films as J. Cousteau: producer, director, and chief cameraman.

For all of Jacques's curiosity, he was bored with school and often got into trouble. Jacques's parents continued to travel a great deal. Not knowing what to do with their troublesome teenager, they sent him to a very strict boarding school. The strong discipline and hard work inspired Jacques to become a good student. "I even studied with a flashlight in bed," said Jacques.

When Jacques graduated in 1929, he wasn't sure whether to become a film director, a radiologist, or a naval officer. Because he also wanted to travel, he decided to enter France's naval academy. His training class was the first to include one year of traveling on a "school ship." He took his camera with him and made a documentary of people and events around the world.

Jacques graduated from the naval academy with the second-highest grades of one thousand students. The navy stationed him at a French base in Shanghai. He continued making movies and shot films of life in China. He then began military pilot training in France.

One night, as Jacques drove a sports car up a foggy mountain road, his lights flickered and the car went out of control. It rolled down a steep hill and he was badly hurt. He still remembers the accident, thinking of how he was "alone at night, bleeding, on a country road, with nobody coming. I thought I was going to die." He remembers looking at the stars and thinking how lucky he had been to have seen so many things in his life.

Jacques didn't die, but he had broken both arms very badly. The doctors said they would have to remove his right arm, but Jacques would not let them. It took him eight months of painful exercises to be able to move just one finger. Two months later he could move two fingers and his wrist. After many months, Jacques was miraculously able to use his right arm again. But he sadly realized he could never be a pilot.

The navy stationed Jacques at Toulon on the Mediterranean Sea. On the beach he met two people who were to become lifelong friends and fellow ocean explorers. One was French Navy Lieutenant Philippe Tailliez. The other was a champion spearfisherman named Frederic Dumas. Philippe encouraged Jacques to swim every day to help strengthen his arms, and Dumas gave Jacques his first pair of goggles to help him see more clearly underwater.

Jacques put the goggles on and dove into the water. Later he said, "Sometimes we are lucky enough to know that our lives have been changed. It happened to me that summer's day when my eyes opened to the world beneath the surface of the sea." Jacques could see "untouched wildlife, a jungle at the border of the sea, never seen by those who floated above." He had discovered a whole new and mysterious world and knew then that he wanted to explore it more.

Most people did not swim at great underwater depths then because there wasn't adequate equipment. The diving suits that were used were bulky and dangerous. Divers wore heavy steel helmets, and air flowed to them through a hose from the ship. Jacques began to experiment with ways to make diving safer and easier. He began to swim on the surface with his head underwater using a small tube to breathe through. He also wore swim fins on his feet to help him move more quickly with less effort. But he wanted to do more.

Jacques had experimented with using air tanks containing different mixes of compressed gases and tried using pure oxygen. He didn't know then that breathing pure oxygen at certain depths could kill him and had a couple of frightening experiences.

Soon Jacques combined his love of filming with his excitement for diving. He wanted very much to share the beauty of the undersea world with others, so he built a waterproof box for his camera. Some of his first underwater black-and-white photos showed Dumas swimming. Jacques met a woman named Simone, and a year later, they were married. Simone loved the ocean and joined Jacques and his friends swimming and diving. Jacques and Simone had two sons, Jean-Michel and Philippe.

Then World War II began, and in 1939 Jacques went to sea on a warship. The Cousteau families and many other people in France struggled to survive during the war. Sometimes food was scarce and Jacques would dive for fish to provide food for his family. The German Nazis took control of France, and Jacques began to think about ways to use his filming and diving skills to help win the war and make the Nazis leave. With his friend Philippe, Jacques worked with a secret underground force against the Nazis. By diving in the harbors, they could look at Nazi ships and find out important information about Nazi equipment.

Jacques also became a spy. In one mission he dressed as a Nazi officer and slipped into Nazi headquarters. There he used a small camera to photograph top-secret papers. After the war, he was awarded medals of honor for his dangerous work.

Jacques was still developing diving equipment. His system now included two air tanks strapped on a diver's back with a hose to bring the air from the tanks to the diver's mouth. What he needed was a special valve to regulate the flow of air. With the help of an engineer named Emile Gagnan, he finally developed a design that allowed people to breathe underwater. Emile and Jacques named their new diving equipment the "aqualung." Later it would be called scuba, short for Self-Contained Underwater Breathing Apparatus.

The excited ocean explorers had much to learn about using the equipment. Diving into very deep water can be dangerous. The cold waters can take away divers' energy and make them too tired to go on. The water pressure makes the air in divers' tanks and lungs act in ways that could be fatal unless certain precautions are taken. If divers come to the surface too fast, they can develop the bends, a serious condition caused when nitrogen is released too quickly in the blood. If they hold their breath as they rise to the surface, their lungs can burst. "Rapture of the deep" is another dangerous condition that occurs on very deep dives. It makes divers feel wonderful but unable to think clearly. In fact, divers with rapture might see things that aren't there or believe they can do dangerous things without being harmed. Jacques, Philippe, and Dumas made more than five hundred dives to solve diving problems.

Jacques and his family loved to dive. Simone was probably the world's first woman scuba diver. Jacques's sons began diving when they were eight and five. The family often dove together and Jacques even had a friend film one of their dives.

At age thirty-nine, Jacques knew that he had the desire and skills to become an ocean explorer. He had spent much of his life in the water already. When the French navy formed the Underwater Research Group to conduct ocean research, Jacques was appointed captain of a marine research vessel, the world's first ship dedicated to exploring beneath the surface of the ocean. With Jacques's experience at sea and his aqualung, he was ready to find many of the answers to questions about the oceans, and he very much wanted to discover the secrets of the "silent world" beneath the water's surface.

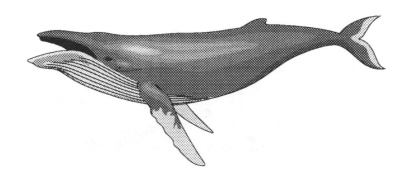

Calypso

Lieutenant Commander Cousteau wanted to pursue his dream of exploring the mysteries of the ocean. In 1950 he was given leave from the navy to do his own research, but he did not have a ship. Jacques knew that a marine research vessel would need to work under many different conditions and must be strongly built. He also knew that she must be able to house various kinds of research equipment.

Jacques looked at ships the British navy was no longer using and when he saw the 140-foot *Calypso,* he knew she would be a good vessel for his work. She had been J-826 as a minesweeper and had also been used as a car ferry. Her name, *Calypso,* means "water nymph." Loel Guinness, an Englishman with the same passion for the sea as Jacques, bought *Calypso* for Jacques's explorations, leased her to him, and she became the vessel that would carry the explorers around the world.

But *Calypso* needed a lot of work to turn her into a research and exploration vessel. Jacques remodeled the living quarters and added special areas for diving equipment. He installed many pieces of research equipment that helped him study oceanography, including the geology, physics, chemistry, life forms, underwater acoustics, and topography of the ocean. He added an underwater observation chamber to *Calypso's* bow ten feet below the waterline. Through the chamber's eight portholes observers can see and film without leaving the ship. Cousteau also added an observation tower on the foredeck to help the crew to see better when navigating through shallow waters or looking for large marine mammals. Preparing *Calypso* for her ocean work took nearly a year. When she was ready to begin her journeys in 1951, there was no other ship like her in the world.

Over the forty years that *Calypso* has explored the oceans, many people have traveled aboard as crew. In the beginning, there was little money to pay a crew. The first trip relied on friends who were invited for the occasion. Jacques later found that there were many people excited about being on his crew. He describes them as "sensitive men, men who have not found happiness or peace in leading an ordinary life." For some, the adventure of the expeditions draws them to *Calypso;* for others it is the solitude and beauty of the sea. For many, the story of *Calypso* is really a story of the human spirit.

Jacques's family, including family dogs, have always been a part of *Calypso* voyages. Simone probably spent more time than Jacques on *Calypso*. Usually the only woman aboard, she helped in many ways. The crew called her their "shepherdess" and she rescued *Calypso* from danger more than once. When Jacques's two sons were ten and twelve years old, they became *Calypso*'s first cabin boys. Although they spent time in boarding schools, they were often aboard *Calypso* and later became leaders in the explorations and filming.

Calypso often carries as many as thirty crew members including scientists, divers, and camera people. Some of the crew have returned to *Calypso* many times, including Jacques's early diving partner Frederic Dumas. Through the years, specialists and scientists from all over the world have joined the crew to conduct research from the famous vessel. Camera operators are an important part of the expeditions and nearly everyone is a diver. Of the many people on Jacques's crews, only three crew members have died during explorations.

Daily life aboard *Calypso* is often exhausting. Sometimes crews work all hours of the day and night. Weather conditions might be too hot, freezing cold, or unpleasantly rainy. There is always work to be done to keep *Calypso* in repair. And, of course, there are always the unpredictable emergencies that come with living on the ocean: storms, squalls, even typhoons. Ship's chores have always been divided among those aboard, and everyone helps with the necessary activities for life aboard *Calypso*. Jacques has one rule: "We must never stop learning." He says, "Our work is to try to understand the sea, its problems, and its exploration. There is, therefore, an endless variety of experiences and a different kind of work every day. And that is the 'adventure' of *Calypso*."

Throughout *Calypso*'s voyages Jacques has produced films, television programs, and books. His adventures and discoveries beneath the surface of the sea have been shared with millions of people through underwater photography. Never before have people around the world been able to share in an explorer's discoveries in quite the same way. The award-winning films and books about *Calypso*'s journeys have also helped people understand the fragile nature of the ocean ecosystem and the dangers it faces from the activities of humans.

Like most explorers before him, Jacques has constantly struggled to find money for his voyages. In the early years he was often paid by businesses and research institutions to use *Calypso* to get information needed for ocean projects. Sometimes organizations such as the National Geographic Society have helped to support *Calypso* voyages. For a number of years, Jacques was the Director of the Oceanographic Museum in the small country of Monaco.

Much of *Calypso*'s work is new, and Cousteau and his crew have had to use their ingenuity to invent new equipment to conduct research and film explorations. Jacques even created an organization to help develop and produce new equipment. Among the most valuable inventions is the *troika*, named after its resemblance to a Russian sled. It can be towed along the ocean bottom at depths of more than twenty-five thousand feet taking photographs of places never before seen by humans.

Calypso still travels all around the world; she has survived the Antarctic cold, typhoons in the Mediterranean Sea, and even gunfire in war zones. Wherever *Calypso*'s voyagers go they seek to understand the ocean using Jacques's motto: "We must go and see for ourselves." Whether they are observing fish, plants, the shape of the ocean bottom, or the remains of a shipwreck, Jacques and *Calypso*'s voyagers have the essential desire that all explorers have expressed: to see and know.

Exploring Life in the Sea

A school of three thousand grunt-fish move together as if they were one creature; an octopus takes refuge in an ancient Mediterranean pottery jar that sits on the ocean bottom; giant turtles creep along an island shore; a sea star lies quietly in the sand four miles below the surface of the sea; a shark appears and then disappears; penguins dance in the long Antarctic day. *Calypso* finds an abundance of fascinating ocean life wherever she goes.

Legends from around the world have spoken of strange sea creatures. Fishers have hunted from boats, searched from the shore, and even ventured into the water with spear or bow in search of food from the sea. But ocean creatures have remained a mystery. Explorers such as Captain Cook, Charles Darwin, and Mary Kingsley collected samples for scientific research by fishing, trolling the ocean floor, and skimming the ocean surface. They brought sea plants and animals from one end of Earth to the other end. But few people had ventured into the depths of the ocean to see the marine inhabitants in their home until Jacques Cousteau. As he once said, "The best way to observe a fish is to become a fish."

In the thirty thousand dives during *Calypso*'s first twenty-five years of research, Cousteau and his crew discovered, named, observed, and photographed marine creatures and plants around the world. Some of their discoveries have been given scientific names in honor of *Calypso*'s expeditions: Calypseus and Cousteaui. One fish was so huge, the alarmed divers nicknamed it a "truckfish" because it seemed as big as a truck. They could not imagine what it was. Finally, it was identified as the largest wrasse that anyone had ever seen.

Though sharks have long held a reputation for their fierceness, Cousteau has found that they rarely attack the divers, and then most often only near the surface of the water. But on one occasion Jacques was reminded of the need to be careful of sharks. Cousteau and Dumas were photographing underwater when a shark appeared. Unconcerned, they continued their work but were surprised when the shark did not swim away. Dumas began to play with the shark while Cousteau took pictures. Suddenly two more of the fifteen-foot creatures appeared and the divers began to worry. They realized that if they swam to the surface the sharks might attack, but the divers were low on air. Using every trick they could think of, Cousteau and Dumas tried to scare the sharks away. Finally, they risked going to the surface to wave for help. When the sharks prepared to attack, the divers quickly dove below again. After a few hair-raising trips up to the surface, help arrived. Cousteau now sends a large cage down with divers when sharks might be near, so divers can get into the cage and be protected from attack.

Calypso's crew is always aware of and interested in life in the unique environment of the sea, and the sea creatures are often just as curious about the divers and their ship. One famous fish who was not camera shy was a rather large grouper the crew named "Jojo." He became friendly with *Calypso*'s crew and would meet divers at the ship's ladder in the morning looking for food treats. Jojo's friendliness became so bothersome during filming that the cameramen had to lock him into the shark cage temporarily while filming other creatures.

Cousteau does not like to capture sea animals or take them from their habitat but has occasionally done so to study them more closely. He had always wanted to study sea lions, so the crew captured two off the coast of South Africa. They were soon named Pepito and Christobal, and they traveled with *Calypso* for seven months. They had their own shelter and swimming pool and eventually dove with the divers, climbing back up the ladder to board the ship.

The camera operators work to capture accurate films of the creatures and their habits. Although much has been learned from their work, there is always more to know. As Jacques says, "There beneath

the keels of our boats lies a little-known universe teeming with life—
a wild marine jungle separated from our civilized world only by the
surface of the sea, an ever-changing boundary that conceals the world
below from our eyes, and has enveloped her in mystery and legend."

Journeys to the Past

Even though people in the past were not able to move freely in the
undersea world, humans have left their mark in the briny deep. The
dangers of currents and weather have brought many ocean vessels to
a watery grave. Jacques Cousteau is fascinated by sunken ships, where
he can feel the drama and mystery of the past brought to life.

Jacques and Dumas had investigated sunken vessels in the navy,
and from the very beginning, *Calypso's* crew explored and filmed
shipwrecks. A new dimension of underwater archaeology emerged
as Cousteau located and investigated sunken ships, submerged cities,
ancient harbors, and even underwater plane wrecks to determine their
history or recover artifacts. This work not only involves diving below
to "see for themselves" but endless hours motoring back and forth
across the water while the ship's sonar scans the bottom. Even before
the crews begin to look in the water, months are spent talking to native
fishermen or searching through libraries to learn the history of shipwrecks, battles, or natural catastrophes.

One of *Calypso's* first shipwreck expeditions was an excavation
near a tiny, barren island off the coast of France. The crew set up a base
camp on the island and named it "Port Calypso." They worked nearly
a full year on the two thousand-year-old sunken Roman ship. Over ten
thousand pieces of ancient pottery and other artifacts were brought to
the surface, classified, and sent to a French museum.

Although the Roman shipwreck excavation was a great success,
tragedy struck *Calypso* when one of her most experienced divers, Jean-
Pierre Servanti, was killed during a dive to retrieve the anchor to the
ship's mooring buoy. With heavy hearts, the crew of the expedition
continued their work.

The magic of discovery creates an air of expectation on *Calypso.*
One of the most exciting archaeological expeditions was a year-long
search for remains of vanished civilizations in the Aegean Sea. The crew
found a three thousand-year-old sunken harbor, a wall of ancient pottery, and an underwater crater filled with ruins. They also discovered
the sixty-year-old wreck of the *Britannic,* sister ship to the famous
Titanic, both of which sank despite claims that they were unsinkable.

There have been disappointments, too. After almost two months of excavating what was believed to be a famous seventeenth-century Spanish ship carrying great treasures, the crew discovered the ship-wreck was instead an eighteenth-century merchant vessel that held little of interest.

Calypso's struggles and discoveries have brought her crew together as a team of explorers. In 1961, Jacques received the National Geographic Society's Gold Medal. The medal was presented to Jacques at the White House by President John F. Kennedy, who described Jacques as "one of the great explorers of an entirely new dimension." The medal shows *Calypso* and her divers and reads, "To Earthbound man he gave the key to the silent world." Cousteau accepted the award by saying, "For me, this is much more than a personal award. It is recognition of a team effort." It is indeed the work of many people on land and sea that has opened the door to the silent world within the ocean waters.

Mapping the Unknown

Look across the land around you and you will see hills and valleys, rocks and flat plains, perhaps even mountains. When we look across the ocean surface we see endless water. But beneath the water is Earth, rock shaped like the land around us. Mountains, hills, and valleys exist below the oceans, too. Before Cousteau invented scuba equipment so humans could actually travel into the ocean's depths, little was known about the shape of the ocean bottom.

Many of *Calypso*'s expeditions involve mapping and researching the geology and topography of the ocean. In the early years, businesses and governments found *Calypso* useful for discovering more about the ocean bottom; oil companies have hired *Calypso* to find mineral and oil deposits and to look for places to lay underwater pipelines.

In one of his first expeditions Jacques explored the deepest valley in the Atlantic Ocean, the Romanche Trench, which is 24,928 feet deep and two miles wide. Cousteau set a record for anchoring a ship in such deep water. Although Jacques would have liked to explore the trench by seeing it for himself, humans cannot survive with scuba alone at this great depth. The pressure of the water would be fatal. So instead, Cousteau lowered photographic equipment to the bottom, where it took remarkable pictures of marine life within the trench. Using additional equipment, the crew mapped the shape of the trench and discovered more about how it had been formed.

To survive at great depths, humans need a very controlled environment that protects them from the intense water pressures and provides the right mixture of gases to breathe. Auguste Piccard developed a deep-diving sphere he called a bathyscaphe. When Cousteau dove to five thousand feet in the large, deep-sea diving sphere he was fascinated by the potential it provided for exploration. He began developing his own smaller design. After much experimentation, a four-ton, saucer-shaped submersible was lowered carefully into the water with no one in it. Suddenly, one of the lines around it snapped and the saucer sank into the ocean beyond human reach. Soon, a second saucer was successfully launched. The small but practical diving saucer has revolutionized underwater exploration by allowing humans to observe and photograph as deep as 1,150 feet in safety. Cousteau's crews have invented smaller versions called "sea fleas" or minisubs.

For a time Cousteau believed that humanity's future in the oceans included communities living and working beneath the sea. People have imagined this possibility for years, and Cousteau keeps a copy of Jules Verne's *Twenty-Thousand Leagues under the Sea* aboard *Calypso* for his crew to read. Cousteau knew of the valuable resources in the ocean—why not farm the sea world and develop other sea industries? At one time he even imagined that artificial gills could be made to allow humans to breathe freely underwater.

As astronauts explored outer space, Cousteau probed deeper into Earth's oceans. He believed that if divers could live underwater, these "oceanauts" would be able to complete a lot of work safely because their bodies would not have to adjust to the new environment each time they surfaced from a dive. So he helped to develop underwater houses that could be used by humans for days, weeks, or months at a time. He studied the effects of men living underwater in experiments called Conshelf I, II, and III. Oceanauts lived below the surface and dove part of the day but also listened to music, played chess, sat under sun lamps, and even had radio and TV. They had frequent visitors from above; Jacques and Simone came down to celebrate their twenty-sixth wedding anniversary on Conshelf II.

Conshelf I was shaped like a large barrel and was anchored to the ocean bottom. Two divers lived in it at thirty-seven feet below the surface for seven days. Conshelf II was made up of four "houses" and could hold seven people. The divers stayed at a depth of thirty-three feet for an entire month, and one group stayed for a week at eighty-two feet with a special gas mixture. Cousteau's film of the Conshelf II experiment was called *World without Sun* and won an Academy Award. In Conshelf III divers lived deeper than ever before: 328 feet below the surface. Cousteau's Conshelf experiments were successful and proved that humans could survive as residents in the ocean depths for a period of time. Later Cousteau decided that living underwater was too strenuous and inconvenient and that humans would always be only visitors in the underwater environment.

On the day that Neil Armstrong and Edwin Aldrin took humanity's first steps on the moon, Jacques noted in his ship's log that *Calypso* diver Raymond Coll was piloting a minisub five hundred feet below the surface of the sea. When Jacques saw the pictures the astronauts sent from the moon of our beautiful blue planet he said, "We can see for ourselves that Earth is a water planet—the only planet to be washed with this vital liquid, so necessary for life. The Earth photograph can drive a second lesson home to us: It can finally make us recognize that the inhabitants of Earth must depend upon and support each other." The Cousteau mission to support the silent undersea world has helped to create a global awareness of the needs of the fragile marine ecosystem on the "water planet."

The Ocean Health Report

When Jacques first dove beneath the ocean's surface in 1936, he was fascinated with its beauty. In the years that followed, he would never cease to find new and exciting things in the oceans. But he would also begin to notice changes that were not part of the natural order of the ecosystem. These changes were caused by human actions and habits.

Covering nearly two-thirds of Earth, the vast oceans have shared their beauty and abundance with Earth's peoples. Humans have taken whales, seals, and fish from its depths and used the animals' bodies for oil, food, and other products. People have carried shiploads of oil across the surface of the sea, sometimes leaking or spilling the oil into the oceans. Huge barges have hauled tons of garbage to sea and dumped it into the water. People are changing the natural patterns of the ocean, clouding the once-clear waters and endangering the life of the plants and creatures of the deep.

From the surface we cannot see below to know the harm that has been caused. But from Jacques Cousteau's underwater view, the changes are obvious. Jacques feels the need to tell people what is happening beneath the water's surface. His films show the changes, and his voice of experience warns of the great losses and fragile nature of the marine world.

Jacques has always had a great respect for the ocean and its creatures. He does not support hurting sea animals; he has actively opposed the use of underwater explosives in ocean mining practices; and he has fought against dumping radioactive wastes into the seas. He has learned the role of the ocean in regulating life upon Earth; he sees that the survival of the planet depends on its creatures living in harmony with each other. For many years, Jacques has kept records of ocean health and monitored the effects of pollution.

As early as 1967, Jacques felt the urgency to give the world an ocean "health report." In 1977 the International Committee for the Scientific Exploration of the Mediterranean accepted Jacques's proposal to devote *Calypso*'s efforts to a survey of the entire Mediterranean area. Jacques conducted a study of environmental conditions that looked at water quality, determined the health of ocean creatures, and investigated the effects of human actions on the ocean. His findings were reported to the United Nations Environmental Program. This survey was used as a model for what was happening or might soon occur in ocean waters around the globe.

The Cousteau Society, a United States organization Jacques formed to help fund his explorations, supported the expensive Mediterranean mission. *Calypso*'s crew also looked for appropriate underwater sites to recommend as underwater parks or biological preserves. Two questions stood out in Jacques's mind as he began his mission: How could such a large body of water change so dramatically and become so contaminated in only forty years? And what needed to be done to restore the oceans to their former vitality? The mission was not easy. *Calypso* visited twelve countries around the Mediterranean. Scientists from each country were delegated to help with the activities and research while *Calypso* was in their territorial waters. But some governments did not cooperate with Jacques fully. Sometimes they would not allow *Calypso* to freely explore, or they limited the expedition's time in the waters near their country. Then the crew would have to work day and night to complete their research.

Calypso returned home with a lot of scientific data. The scientists could see that pollution had not created real danger in most parts of the Mediterranean, but Jacques knew that the gradual disappearance of marine wildlife was not good. The expedition helped to identify which actions people would have to change to protect the oceans. They found that certain fishing practices, changing the course of rivers or building artificial banks along shorelines, and dumping wastes or toxic chemicals into the oceans created an imbalance in the ocean ecosystem. While changing human habits would not be easy, it was obvious that human needs and the rhythms of the undersea world must find greater harmony.

Calypso continues to monitor the health of Earth's waters in the Arctic and Antarctic, the Pacific and Atlantic oceans, the many seas, and even the world's great rivers. Cousteau's missions now include the use of a new ship called *Alcyone,* which uses diesel fuel and a new type of wind sail in an effort to reduce fossil fuel consumption. Cousteau's projects are dedicated to understanding and protecting the environment. The Cousteau Society still produces films and books while organizing expeditions around the world. Jacques Cousteau was eighty-two years old in 1992. He continues to dive in warm waters and has designed a diving regulator that meets the breathing needs of older divers. His life's goal is still to explore; he is a man who does not look back but continually presses on to new experiences. When asked what place in the world is his favorite he is likely to reply that it is wherever he will go next.

Jacques Cousteau's dedication to the ocean comes from his love of the mysterious underwater world. He realizes that one of the most important roles of his expeditions is to share knowledge and experiences. Jacques supports world peace and the protection of the environment as a way of saving the world, "not only for ourselves, but for our children and their children." He has outlined a Bill of Rights for Future Generations that stresses the importance of giving each generation the "right to an uncontaminated and undamaged Earth." The many people who have been involved in Jacques's expeditions share his philosophy that "we must go and see for ourselves." But the Cousteau crews are also the eyes into the sea for all people of Earth and they are the voice that speaks for the silent underwater world.

Exploring Further

- Read Jules Verne's *Twenty-Thousand Leagues under the Sea,* Greek and Roman sea myths, or other stories about living beneath the sea. Make up your own story about an undersea community.

- Find examples of art whose subject is the sea, such as some Japanese prints, coastal Native American art, Paul Klee's *Fish Magic,* some of Winslow Homer's paintings, or *Three Worlds* by M. C. Escher. Make your own sea drawings and create a sea art exhibit with your classmates.

- Interview a scuba diver, an oceanographer, a government water resource specialist, a sailor, an ecologist, a marine biologist, or another person involved with water. Ask for their thoughts about the health of our water resources and report back to the class.

- Find out which sea creatures inhabit deep ocean trenches, coral reefs, Arctic waters, tropical shore zones, or Nordic fjords. With a friend, make a mural of one of these ocean ecosystems.

- Make a list of ocean fish, mammals, or plants that have become extinct or are currently endangered. How can people help keep endangered species from becoming extinct? Make a list of suggestions and share them with the class.

- Find out what Jacques Cousteau's Bill of Rights for Future Generations includes. Write your own Bill of Rights for Future Generations.

- Make a list of resources humans use from the ocean. (Include items that use seaweed products such as algin and carrageenan.) Make of list of what humans put into the ocean waters. What are the problems caused by human activities? Share your lists and thoughts with the class.

- Find out more about underwater archaeology. Research the story of a shipwreck.

- Explore the stories surrounding the lost continent of Atlantis, including Jacques Cousteau's attempts to solve the mystery.

- Some sea creatures communicate by sound underwater. Explore ways that dolphins, whales, lobsters, beavers, and other water mammals communicate through sound waves. How has human technology used these same ideas for navigation and research? Write a short report.

- With three or four friends, develop a code of simple clicking, clucking, snapping, or whistling sounds to communicate about food, danger, or travel directions. Find out about pilot whale communication techniques to help you. Share your code with the class.

- Find sea music such as Irish sea chants, Claude Debussy's *La Mer* or "Sirenes" from Nocturnes, or John Denver's "Calypso." Play your music for the class. What feeling or idea does the music express?

Explorations into Outer Space

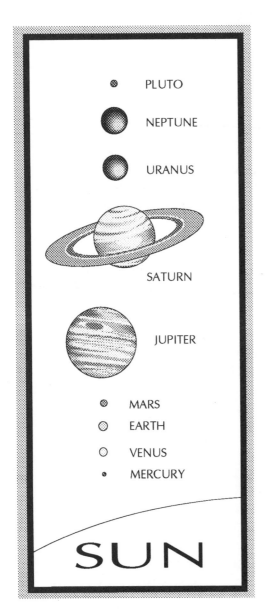

PLUTO

NEPTUNE

URANUS

SATURN

JUPITER

MARS

EARTH

VENUS

MERCURY

SUN

Columbus, Kingsley, Amundsen, and Cousteau changed humanity's perception of the areas they explored. Although they were aided by many individuals, their visions were unique. Because the success of the space program cannot be attributed to an individual, in this section we include a history of space exploration before discussing Edgar Mitchell, a representative of many talented people.

Early Years

"That's one small step for man . . . one giant leap for mankind." These words, spoken by Neil Armstrong, marked one of the greatest accomplishments of humankind—the first step on the moon. As with most explorations, preparations for this journey began many years before. On October 4, 1957, the first voyage into outer space was made not by a human but by a small metal ball shot several hundred miles above Earth. The basketball-sized satellite was the first humanmade object to be placed in Earth's orbit. The Soviet Union named their satellite *Sputnik*, meaning "fellow traveler." The Space Age had begun.

Spaceships and Astrochimps

For the first time in the history of exploration, the explorers who went into unknown places were not human. Instead, they were scientific instruments. The creaking wooden ships that had carried many earlier explorers were replaced by strangely shaped capsules fired forcefully into the air. The success of these expeditions did not rely on the physical abilities or clever thinking of the leader but on the science and technology that went into building space capsules and equipment—the work of entire nations involved in the production, support, and development of a space program.

Before humans could travel in space, there was much to learn about the environment they would be entering. Brave explorers of Earth had faced many dangers, but space presented entirely new challenges. No longer did explorers worry about winds and ocean currents. Now they must worry about the effects of gravity, the lack of an atmosphere, the loneliness and void of space.

Many questions were asked: Could living beings survive the pain of lift-off? How would people react to being weightless? Could people live and work in space? How long could someone survive in space? What kind of space suits would living beings need to wear to provide life support and protection? Dogs, mice, monkeys, chimpanzees, rabbits, frogs, and plants would lead the way into space and provide scientists with information on life support in this new environment.

In November 1957, one month after *Sputnik* had successfully orbited Earth, the Soviets launched *Sputnik II*. Inside the 1,120-pound capsule was the first living being to orbit Earth: Laika, a female fox terrier. The fourteen-pound dog had just enough room to sit, stand, and lie down. Food and air were provided and she was monitored for the effects of space travel by scientific instruments attached to her body. Though Laika died when her air supply ran out after one week, she paved the way for human explorers.

Meanwhile, in Project Manhigh, the United States used hot-air balloons to research the effects of exposure to cosmic and solar radiation and to gather information about the outer-space environment. The project lasted four years and sent a human passenger aloft in a pressurized capsule in 1957. One year later, the United States formed the National Aeronautics and Space Administration. NASA's first projects included sending the unmanned spacecraft *Explorer* into orbit around Earth and launching four *Pioneer* rockets toward the moon. Project Mercury, named after the fleet-footed Greek messenger of the gods, was designed to experiment with life-support equipment. Three of the successful launches carried living beings: rhesus monkeys Sam and Miss Sam, and a chimpanzee named Ham. All three space animals returned to Earth safely and in good health. One of the most famous astroanimals was a squirrel monkey named Miss Baker, who stayed healthy and happy for the twenty years she lived at the Alabama Rocket Center following her 1959 space flight.

People in Space

Fifty miles above Earth the atmosphere thins and outer space begins. Past this boundary, there is only darkness, and the sun, moon, and stars can always be seen. Night and day as we know them do not exist. There is no food, no water, not even any air—just blackness and deadly cold. Dangerous radiation is everywhere, because there is no atmosphere to block out cosmic rays. Bits of rock called micrometeoroids fly by like bullets. With no gravity in space, nothing has weight. If you were in space, your blood would flow upward from your feet toward your head. Your legs and waist would get thinner while your face and arms puffed up. You would even get a bit taller. You would have the sniffles and you might feel sick and dizzy for a while. Your heart, bones, and muscles would get weaker.

Who would be the first people sent into space? What skills and abilities did a space traveler need? Courage, physical health and strength, a sense of calm in the face of danger, desire and willingness to face the unknown, and the ability to understand technical information all seemed very important. Where would the space programs find what one Air Force general called "ordinary supermen"? Both the Soviet Union and the United States chose jet pilots. Those who tested and flew jet planes were faced with constant danger and understood how to handle it. They flew at high altitudes at extremely fast speeds and had to make critical decisions instantly.

The Soviets called their space travelers *cosmonauts,* from the Greek word *kosmos* meaning universe or world. The United States' first astronauts, or "travelers to the stars," were required to be under forty years old, to have flown a minimum of fifteen hundred hours in a jet, to have an engineering background, and to be shorter than 5'11" in order to fit in small space capsules. Both astronauts and cosmonauts went through a great deal of training, which included use of instruments, wilderness survival, physics, communications, astronomy, rocket propulsion, meteorology, space medicine, and spacecraft design.

On April 12, 1961, the Soviet "traveler of the universe" Yuri Gagarin became the first man to orbit Earth. Yuri was launched 200 miles above Earth in a rocket called the *Vostok.* Orbiting at 18,000 miles an hour, the *Vostok* made a single orbit of Earth in one hour and eighteen minutes.

The spacecraft then automatically fired retro-rockets, which slowed it enough to make the craft drop from orbit and return to Earth.

One of the most dangerous parts of a space journey is the reentry into the thick layer of air around Earth. During the rapid fall of a space capsule to Earth, friction with the air creates intense heat on the outside of the capsule. Without a heat shield, space capsules would burn up on reentry. As Yuri's space capsule tumbled to Earth at 17,000 miles per hour, flames broke out along the outside of the ship. The temperature on the outside was 2,000 degrees Fahrenheit, but inside the cabin was cool. After a few moments the flames died out. The pull of gravity at the speed Yuri's capsule fell is ten times that of normal Earth gravity. This G-force made the 150-pound Yuri feel like a falling 1,500-pound brick. Earth came closer and closer until giant parachutes automatically released and slowed the fall of the *Vostok*. Yuri was ejected and his own parachute brought him to the ground.

The Soviet government had not told the public about Yuri's historic journey into space. Even his mother did not know that he was in space until he was actually orbiting Earth. When Yuri landed in a plowed field on his return, two farm women stared in amazement at the human figure in a strange orange suit and white helmet. When one of the women bravely asked Yuri if he had come from space, the cosmonaut smiled and replied, "Yes."

Twenty-three days later, the United States sent Alan Shepard into space and then Virgil "Gus" Grissom. Though there were some difficulties with reentry, these flights were mostly successful and showed that humans could enter space and return safely. Longer flights were attempted. John Glenn was the first United States astronaut to orbit Earth. To honor his journey, the entire population of Perth, Australia, turned on their lights as Glenn passed over Australia at midnight. The bright glowing spot below was a welcome reminder of the many people on Earth who eagerly watched his adventure.

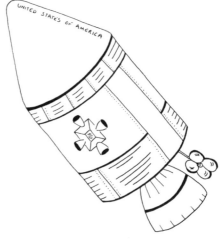

In early space flights, astronauts were not allowed to control their spacecraft. For many of the astronauts who had piloted jets, simply being a passenger in a space capsule was frustrating. Spacecraft control was handled from a mission control center. Emergency manual control was possible but had not been needed until John Glenn's flight. An equipment malfunction forced him to assume control before he reentered Earth's atmosphere. If he failed to reenter the atmosphere at the right angle, Glenn knew that his ship might bounce off the thick atmosphere and end up orbiting Earth forever. Or he might be shot off within the atmosphere like a shooting star and burn to ashes. As John Glenn was thinking about his options, Mission Control informed him that his heat shield appeared to be loose. If it did not work, his ship would burn up on reentry no matter how he entered the atmosphere.

With no choice, Glenn fired his retro-rockets and headed for Earth. As he collided with the thick atmosphere around Earth, the capsule shook violently. Tremendous G-forces pushed on his chest and John Glenn struggled to keep control of the ship. He could hear a hissing noise from outside and see burning pieces of the space capsule fly past. As he was beginning to think he would soon burn up, John suddenly found himself looking at blue skies and gently floating beneath parachutes. The heat shield had held together and Glenn had kept control of the ship.

While the United States learned about orbiting and reentry, the Soviets began to explore long journeys into space. They accomplished space capsule rendezvous, which is bringing two spacecraft close to one another in orbit. And much to the surprise of the United States, one of the cosmonauts was a woman named Valentina Tereshkova.

Tereshkova was twenty-six when she became the first woman in space. She had dreamed of being a cosmonaut. When she was sixteen, Tereshkova began working in a tire factory and went to school in the evenings. She became a cotton-spinning technologist in 1961 and was the head of a parachute club. When Tereshkova heard the Soviet Union was looking for women cosmonauts, she volunteered for service and became one of the first five women trained for space travel. Tereshkova flew in the *Vostok VI* flight, circling Earth forty-eight times. The United States would not train a woman astronaut for another twenty years.

In 1961, President Kennedy resolved to put a United States astronaut on the moon. It would take many years and experiments, many successes and failures before this would happen. During this time the United States also developed the Space Transportation System, or space shuttles, to make space travel less costly and easier. These reusable spacecraft are shot into space by rocket boosters but land much like airplanes. The United States has successfully flown many shuttles with only one serious disaster occurring when seven astronauts were killed in the explosion of the *Challenger*. Space shuttles offer great potential for future human space activity. Satellites can be repaired, sent into space, or retrieved with a shuttle. Even private industry has become involved in shuttle programs.

Future ideas for space include tourism, space manufacturing, a moon base, traveling space stations, exploration of other planets and galaxies, and . . . ? The ideas go as far as human imagination can take them. Many people are opposed to the great cost of human exploration of space, and some feel human ethics need to be more fully developed before we expand to new horizons. Yet for others, the call of the unknown draws the human spirit ever outward and beyond into new areas for exploration.

Apollo to the Moon: 1961–1969

The Apollo moon-landing expedition required careful planning and practice. There was much to learn about the lunar surface, moon orbits, and how to maneuver spacecraft. The first Apollo flights tested equipment but were unmanned. Then, with astronauts aboard, *Apollo 8* orbited the moon, *Apollo 9* practiced flying and docking the LM (lunar module) and the CSM (command/service module) in Earth orbit, and *Apollo 10* practiced the entire moon trip except for the actual landing. The mission to the moon was ready; *Apollo 11* would attempt the landing.

Three astronauts were chosen for the landing, all known for their superior piloting abilities: Neil Armstrong, Edwin "Buzz" Aldrin, and Michael Collins. The night before the launch the famous rocket designer Werner von Braun, who was responsible for much of NASA's success, commented, "What we will have attained when Neil Armstrong steps down upon the moon is a completely new step in the evolution of man. For the first time, life will leave its planetary cradle, and the ultimate destiny of man will no longer be confined to these familiar continents that we have known so long."

In July 1969, *Apollo 11* was successfully launched and headed for the moon at 25,000 miles per hour. During the journey, the spacecraft constantly rotated to help keep the outside cool. Every two minutes the sun, Earth, and the moon could be seen at the same time through *Apollo 11*'s windows. By the third day the crew entered the orbit of the moon, and Earth was just a tiny ball in the sky.

Neil Armstrong and Buzz Aldrin entered the LM, the *Eagle*, and began the sixty-mile descent to the moon's surface. As they approached the surface, they directed the LM to flat ground in an area called the Sea of Tranquility. Six hours later they opened the hatch, set up the television cameras, and the world watched breathlessly as Neil Armstrong stepped onto the moon.

The United States flag, supported so that it looked as if it were waving in the windless moon air, was firmly planted on lunar soil. For two historic hours, Armstrong and Aldrin moved about the surface of the moon, carefully at first in the different gravity, but eventually leaping across the moon's surface like kangaroos. Upon returning home, the explorers spent their first seventeen days in quarantine to make sure they had not brought unknown bacteria with them from the moon.

In the next three years, five moon flights would land ten more astronauts on the moon. Nearly a ton of lunar rock and soil would be collected, some of which was 4.6 billion years old. A new vision of Earth would be shared with humanity. Among the space travelers who would help others recognize the significance of this vision was United States astronaut Edgar Mitchell.

Edgar Mitchell

1930–

Early Years

Five-year-old Edgar Mitchell watched in wonder as a barn-storming airplane rose from his family's farm and flew overhead. Thirty-five years later he would feel the bone-jarring sensation of a Saturn rocket lift him into outer space toward the moon. But Edgar would set and reach many goals before he would become the sixth man to walk on the moon. His accomplishments would follow from the lesson he learned as a child—to "do the best you can." Edgar was born on September 17, 1930, and grew up on cattle ranches in Texas and New Mexico. Edgar's grandfather was a wheat farmer whose livelihood was destroyed by the wind and erosion of the dust bowls during the Depression. With his three sons, Edgar's grandfather drove railroad spikes for one dollar a day to earn the nine dollars needed to buy a heifer calf. From this single cow, the Mitchell family built a large cattle-ranching business, including farm machinery dealerships and feed farms. The Mitchells proved to be good farmers with determination and no fear of hard work.

For Edgar, the farms provided an outlet for his intense curiosity about how things worked. There was never a shortage of equipment that needed to be repaired, and as a young child Edgar learned about machines by watching his father fix them. By the time Edgar was nine he was driving tractors and teams of horses.

Edgar's interest in flying grew as he watched airplanes from Walker Air Force Base in their flight patterns over one of the Mitchell feedlots. In his few spare moments, Edgar built model airplanes and read about Charles Lindbergh's epic flight across the Arctic and Richard Byrd's air explorations at the South Pole. He also read popular adventure stories and the real-life adventures of explorers such as Lewis and Clark.

Edgar's Uncle George was an amateur pilot who thrilled the young boy with his first airplane ride in a J3 Piper Cub. Spurred on by his fascination for flying, Edgar washed airplanes at a local airport to pay for flying lessons. When he was thirteen, Edgar made his first solo flight and became a licensed pilot.

Edgar's parents recognized his mechanical ability and encouraged him to study engineering in college. Shortly after he graduated, Edgar joined the United States Navy and attended flight school. As a navy pilot, Edgar was stationed near Okinawa and flew in the South China Sea. His only experience with air battle occurred during his last mission. On his return from patrol duty, Edgar was attacked by two Korean fighter planes. He evaded them by flying at a slow speed near the water, where the Korean's fast planes were forced to leave him untouched.

When *Sputnik* successfully orbited Earth and the Space Age began, Edgar decided that he wanted to be among the future space explorers. At age twenty-seven, Edgar was too young to be accepted into NASA's astronaut training program, but he set about gaining the experience he knew he would need. Edgar returned to college, this time to get his doctorate in engineering. He attended one of the first doctoral programs designed to develop a space career and graduated in Aeronautics and Astronautics from Massachusetts Institute of Technology. Because of his extensive background in engineering, Edgar also taught in the program.

Edgar applied to NASA's astronaut program twice but was not accepted. Although he was more highly qualified than most applicants in engineering, he needed more flight time. Reassigning to Edwards Air Force Base, Edgar accumulated a total of 2,000 hours of jet flight time. Finally in 1966, nine years after he had decided to be an astronaut, Edgar was accepted by NASA.

The Journey to Outer Space: 1966–1971

Space travel involves complex equipment that requires technical training to understand and operate. Edgar spent five years working on NASA ground crews to train for his first space flight. Edgar and astronaut Fred Haise were instrumental in the engineering development of the lunar module. Edgar served as a member of the astronaut support crew for *Apollo 9* and as backup lunar module pilot on *Apollo 10*. Finally, he was scheduled as a crew member for the *Apollo 13* flight. But crew assignments were rotated and Edgar's friend Fred Haise became the lunar module pilot for the flight while Edgar was rescheduled for *Apollo 14* and would serve as ground crew for *Apollo 13*.

Fifty-five hours into the *Apollo 13* flight, an oxygen tank exploded aboard the command/service module, rupturing the tank and blowing a panel from the side of the service module. The crew was forced to activate the lunar module support systems and move into the tiny vehicle. There would be no moon landing. Mission control and the astronauts focused instead on finding a way to bring the men safely home to Earth. Edgar went immediately to the lunar module simulator at mission control and began to invent and test procedures the *Apollo 13* crew would need. The lives of the astronauts were at stake.

It would take the lunar module three and one-half days to reach Earth. Edgar worked constantly with only a few hours' rest. As soon as he felt comfortable with a procedure, the information would be sent by radio for Fred to try. People around the world anxiously waited. Fortunately, the sturdy lunar module successfully crossed the cold, black gap between Earth and her moon. The temperature in the spacecraft dropped to near freezing, and the astronauts wore as much warm clothing as the confined space in the Aquarius would allow. Still, they were too uncomfortable to sleep well.

Once in Earth's orbit the astronauts released the badly damaged service module and prepared the command module for reentry. Would the cold of the last few days keep the command module from functioning now? Miraculously, all of CM's systems worked and the lunar module was set adrift in space. The world responded with tears of joy and excitement as the *Apollo 13* crew safely descended to Earth's surface.

It was now Edgar Mitchell's turn to explore outer space. The first United States astronaut to enter space, forty-seven-year-old Alan Shepard, was scheduled as *Apollo 14* Commander and Stuart Roosa as pilot of the CSM. Edgar Mitchell was the lunar module pilot. On January 31, 1971, the *Apollo 14* crew entered outer space on a trajectory for the moon. For Edgar Mitchell, fear was not a problem, because every aspect of a space flight is practiced over and over on Earth until it becomes routine. This extensive training and practice had given him great confidence in himself and the *Apollo 14* team.

For this moon flight the CSM moved into an orbit that brought it closer to the lunar surface than any prior Apollo mission. Alan Shepard described the stark moonscape as looking "like a plaster mold that somebody has dusted with grays and browns." The crew had named their lunar module *Antares* after the largest star in the Scorpio constellation; it was also the star Alan and Ed used for navigation as they directed the lunar module to the Fra Mauro Crater. Ed's years of work and preparation were fully rewarded as he became the sixth human to step onto the lunar surface. Ed and Alan stayed on the moon for thirty-three hours, longer than any human up to that time.

Ed and Alan were kept busy on the moon setting up scientific experiments and collecting data. Solar-wind collection and seismic experiments were conducted. The Fra Mauro Crater contained geologic information scientists hoped would help explain the moon's formation. Ed and Alan explored Fra Mauro by walking across a portion of it, farther than any human had yet walked on the moon. Their observations of the area were recorded, and they collected ninety-eight pounds of lunar surface samples. To carry tools and samples, the astronauts used a mobile equipment transporter (MET). This was the first time a vehicle with wheels had been used on the moon. Basically a handcart, it was probably much like the first carts used by humans on Earth in ancient times.

Upon returning to the *Antares*, Alan surprised Mission Control with another moon first: he brought out a golf ball and used a sampling tool to hit the first golf stroke on lunar soil. Throwing an equipment handle like a javelin, Edgar threw the handle farther than Alan's golf shot and, with these parting shots, the two astronauts piloted the *Antares* back to Stu Roosa in the CSM. The *Apollo 14* moon mission was complete and the astronauts began their journey home. The experience that followed marked a turning point in Edgar Mitchell's life. In the following section he tells about his journey into inner space.

The Journey to Inner Space: 1971
by Edgar Mitchell

In the cabin of *Apollo 14,* Alan Shepard, Stu Roosa, and I have just left lunar orbit after a very exciting, fulfilling, and successful exploration of the lunar surface. The rugged moonscape is slowly becoming smaller as we watch out the cabin window on our way home. We are happy, relaxed, and very tired. We have not eaten in twelve hours or slept in twenty-two hours. The crew tasks are light, giving us a chance to rest, to recover from sore muscles, and bask in the satisfaction of a mission well done.

I take this opportunity to get a glimpse of Earth. It is a rare event and I feel privileged to be one of only a few persons in all history to leave the planet and view it from deep space. It is a beautiful little planet—blue and white—set in the black emptiness of the universe with billions of bright stars as a backdrop. I can see stars that we see from Earth only with a telescope. We now know that Earth is only a small planet that circles an average-sized sun, way out on the spiral arm of a rather ordinary galaxy that is only one of millions of galaxies. Space is so big that distances are measured in light-years, not in miles or even millions of miles.

In my adult life I have been an engineer, a scientist, a test pilot, a naval officer. I have worked daily with mathematics, technical equipment, and the hard facts of my profession, as well as the realities of war. But like many I have pondered questions that have troubled humankind for thousands of years—questions such as Why am I here? What is the purpose of human life? How did the universe begin? Are the planets and stars really formed by an accidental collision of bits of matter or is there much, much more? Is there a divine plan that humankind and the other inhabitants of planet Earth are carrying out? These were the very questions that fueled the fire of human curiosity and led us to overcome gravitational pull and carry out the great adventure to walk on the moon.

I contemplated these questions while looking at the magnificence of planet Earth—floating in the vastness of space like a grain of sand in a cosmic sea. And as I did so, an experience occurred that completely calmed my mind on these troublesome issues. I experienced a oneness with life and I knew in one instant that certainly life had purpose. I knew that Earth was only one of millions—perhaps billions—of planets with intelligent life all playing a role in evolution. Any question about our destiny or the nature of the universe suddenly melted away. It was as though my awareness reached out to touch the furthest star and I was aware of being a part of the entire universe. For one brief instant I felt how perfect, how loving, how orderly was this universe that we inhabit.

However, as I continued to gaze at Earth, the sense of oneness changed to a feeling of deep despair. It was the darkest, blackest emotional pain I have ever felt. As I thought about the humans who lived on my blue planet, I saw them behaving like ancient warring tribes—fighting over food and territorial rights like spoiled children fighting over favorite toys. How painful to know that beneath Earth's blue atmosphere and white clouds were my people, living in disharmony with each other.

These thoughts were interrupted as my duties aboard *Apollo 14* demanded that I function as a member of our homeward-bound crew. However, for the next thirty hours, the experience was repeated in my moments of rest. There was the overwhelming feeling of oneness with the universe and a sense of human purpose, followed by despair at the recognition that we were hurting only ourselves as we continued our destructive behaviors.

To return successfully to Earth the three of us aboard *Apollo 14* had to conserve our spaceship's resources and work as a team. It made me think of Buckminster Fuller's description of the Earth as a spaceship for her people. The Earth is all we have—the spaceship that supports our life. It was quite apparent in the view from space how tiny, fragile, and limited Earth is. For the planet to survive and provide growth and well-being of her inhabitants, humankind must rise to the challenge of cooperating as a crew on spaceship Earth.

For tens of thousands of years we have roamed the Earth fighting for survival in a harsh environment, protecting ourselves and our possessions, and warring with those who seemed to threaten. For generations humans have believed that power and force were the only workable tools to motivate people and shape the world. We are now beginning to understand that such beliefs create only hatred and distress—the opposite of what we want. Human beings spend their time fighting each other to gain their ends instead of cooperating and finding a satisfactory life-style through understanding. We do not recognize our God-given gifts of intelligence, intuition, and creativity—or the guiding spirit within us that makes humankind great and could enable us to rise above our more base instincts.

In earlier times, our limited numbers and primitive tools prevented us from endangering the planet. We were a pastoral agricultural community dependent upon cooperation with nature for survival. But in the twentieth century our growing population and explosion of scientific knowledge have changed our world into an industrialized, computerized, and technical society. We were, and still are, using non-renewable resources at an alarming rate. The data we now have tell us we will find ourselves out of these resources within the next century if we continue to use them this fast. We now have the power and knowledge to control life on Earth, but have we the wisdom and sense of purpose necessary to control the technological genie we have set free? How can Earth support a civilization determined to destroy itself by the misuse of our planet's great gifts?

Long after I returned to Earth in February 1971, I pondered the ancient questions of life and tried to understand the experience that occurred as I returned from the moon. I sought the counsel of wise and gifted people: ancient and present-day scholars, mystics, philosophers, scientists, and theologians. I wanted not only to understand their insights but also to find workable solutions to our human crisis. I set out to find what potential humankind had for meaningful and productive change. What is it we could become if we but dare?

The sciences of medicine, biology, chemistry, and traditional psychology describe our bodies— our fragile physical machinery. But what are we really? Is our nature truly just flesh and bones? How are we different from our animal neighbors? As humans, we have the capacity for self-reflection, the ability to think our thoughts, to dream our dreams, and to have our visions of a better world— a peaceful place to live.

Thoughts, dreams, and visions alone do not change the world. However, they can inspire us to a new sense of ourselves. This change in consciousness has happened to thousands of people in every walk of life during every age. Those who experience this change in thinking have been able to rise above previous beliefs and to see themselves and the world in a different way.

Astronauts are trained to be objective and scientific. Yet almost every one of us had powerful, moving experiences upon seeing Earth from deep space. We were privileged to see Earth and the cosmos from a totally new perspective. I now firmly believe that we can solve the ills of our planet only with an understanding of our consciousness and a willingness to perceive things differently.

Belief system is everything. What we see, think, and do corresponds to what we believe we are. Only as we change our view of ourselves and our belief about our reality will we start to see what we can become. If we want to create a peaceful, abundant universe we have to think and to live that way. We will have to become as dynamic as the universe around us and replace old ideas with new ones.

An explorer is a person who is curious about something. Artists are explorers because they are creating something out of nothing. Scientists are explorers because they are searching the unknown. Explorers look for what has never been done before.

In today's world everyone has the opportunity to be
an explorer because the environment is constantly
changing around us. It is a new world every day.
And at no other time has it been so obvious that
humans are shaping—for better or worse—the future
of their planet. The most important lesson that
humanity presently needs to learn is to take responsibility for itself, to understand that we can't look to
anybody else as the cause of our problems or successes. To survive, humans will all have to become
explorers. We will have to explore ourselves, our
view of the universe, and ways we can work together
as a crew aboard spaceship Earth. The choice is ours.

In 1973 Edgar Mitchell founded and served as first president of
the Institute of Noetic Sciences. Noetic, as he describes it, refers to the
"total set of means we have for gaining knowledge, including intuition." His purpose in founding the institute was to explore the realms
of consciousness and the human spirit systematically through scientific
research and education. The next frontier is mind and spirit.

Exploring Further

■ Explore how the Chinese made rockets more than eight hundred
years ago. Look at pictures of both real and fictional spacecrafts.
Design your own, determine its mission, and give it a name.

■ Find out about behind-the-scenes space flight personnel. Make a
list of the various mission control jobs and the technical positions
involved in research and development at NASA.

■ Research the possibility of space settlements. Find out what is being
planned now and what people have imagined in the past. Draw a
picture of your vision of a space settlement.

■ Conduct a survey by interviewing ten people about humanity's role
in space. Ask at least three questions, including *Should we continue to
explore outer space?* Compile your survey results and share them with
the class.

■ Many artists have drawn images of space from real photographs
and from their imaginations. See if you can find space art by Paul
Doherty, Paul Hudson, or others. Use watercolors, acrylic paints,
or oil pastels to create your own space art.

- Explore legends of travel to space: the Greek myth of Daedalus and Icarus, Jules Verne's *From Earth to the Moon*, Mayan legends, or contemporary science fiction such as *Star Trek* or Isaac Asimov's stories. Write your own short story about travel in space.

- With a friend, build a command module from a large appliance box. Build in your own controls, computer, and other equipment. Paint the outside and create a cassette recording of your launch.

- Find out what is meant by space junk. How much is there? What problems does it cause? How do we protect against it? Write a report and share it with the class.

- Study the history of Soviet Union space flight. Make a time line of United States and Soviet Union "firsts" in space.

- Find out about the requirements to be an astronaut or space shuttle crew member. Write a description of astronaut and shuttle crew duties.

- The surface of Earth, the "water planet," is two-thirds ocean. Find photographs and descriptions of Mars, Venus, or Pluto. Write your own description of one of them. Why can't they support human life?

- The Freedom space station is a joint project by Canada, Europe, Japan, and the United States. Find out more about it and write a report for the class.

- From clay, make a model of the moon. Add small flags where United States astronauts have landed.

III EXPLORING THROUGH TIME

Activities: Exploring the Past

- Find three definitions of explorers from reference books: dictionaries, encyclopedias, or books on explorers. Ask five people for their definition of an explorer. Compile your results and share them with the class.

- Use the five explorers in this guide to help determine the reasons people have explored in the past. Make a mind map using words and symbols that illustrate past exploration goals and include what you think humans will explore next.

- How did the five explorers in this guide prepare themselves for their journeys? Make lists of how and where each of them got information that helped them decide what things to take and how to travel. Also include the scientific studies each explorer needed to complete before making his or her journey.

- Many explorers had to invent new equipment to survive in the harsh or foreign environments they explored. Make lists of the various inventions created by each explorer in this guide.

- Compare the various ways explorers have gotten the money and equipment needed for their expeditions. Make a chart of explorers and their funding sources.

- Compare the vehicles used by each of the five explorers in this guide. As a class project, make clay or papier mâché models of the different vehicles and write brief descriptions of them. Display them in the school library.

- Write a guided imagery that reflects the environment explored by one of the people in this book. Include descriptive words that bring the landforms, colors, people, animals, climate, and feelings alive. Select music of the appropriate native group or sounds that set the mood for the feeling of the environment. Read your imagery to the class with the music playing softly in the background. Ask students to close their eyes while you read. When you are done ask them to draw or paint a picture that illustrates the imagery. Continue to play the music while the class draws. Share pictures and ask each student to explain what stood out most in the imagery.

- List the significant contributions of the five explorers in this guide to human knowledge. Include categories of geography, science, cultural understanding, and politics.

- What personal characteristics do explorers seem to have that make them successful in their goals? Make a mind map or list of the common traits.

- How do you think the explorers in this book felt when they realized their goals? Find quotations or descriptions by the explorers that share their feelings. Read them to the class.

- Before the five explorers began their expeditions, previous explorers had attempted similar journeys or had provided information that helped these five explorers complete their missions. Select one of the explorers in this guide and note people and expeditions that contributed to his or her success. Show your results in a time line, a series of illustrations, or a written report.

- Reflect on the impact of explorers on the native peoples in the lands they reached. Make a list of positive and negative consequences of the meeting of different cultures.

- Research the role of women in exploration. How unusual was it for Mary Kingsley to become an explorer? Find out about other women explorers, including women who traveled with their husbands on expeditions, explored and climbed mountain peaks, explored the ocean depths, worked with anthropologic missions, or explored in air or space vehicles. Write a short biography of a woman explorer and draw an illustration of one of the incidents in her journeys.

- Research a native culture and find out what explorations they may have made. Consider native Americans, Africans, Australians, or island peoples. Write a report on one of them.

Activities: Exploring the Present

- Select a country that interests you. Explore it through books, videos, music, art, and personal experiences of someone who has traveled there. Write a short report that includes examples of art, music, and personal stories.

- Think of someone in your area who has done something you admire. Ask if you can conduct an interview. Find out how this person became interested in and learned about his/her special area of knowledge or expertise. Tape record your interview or write a short biography and share it with the class. Perhaps include a photo.

- Find out about the history of your area. Who explored it and what did they do? Who are the native peoples in your area? Write a short report about the exploration and history of your area.

- Find out from your parents if a family vacation or one-day outing is planned. If so, ask them if you can help plan the "expedition." With their help, chart your proposed route and determine daily proposed mileage. How far will you go in a day? What will you need to take? What do you want to see or find out on your journey? Who will go with you? Make a written plan and share it with the class.

The Discovery Journey: Techniques for Teachers

The Discovery "Road Map"

A "road map" that highlights the important steps along a learning journey will provide students with an understanding of the process of exploration into curriculum subjects. It also encourages personal responsibility in learning. Some students will appreciate the use of symbols and pictures in a road map more than an outline. Use a road map for any classroom subject to create a meaningful visual of the exploration process of learning.

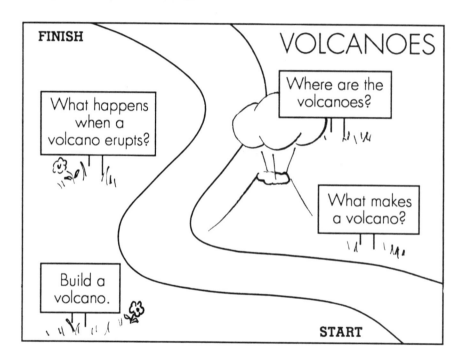

Information Images

The ability to describe and observe develops the processes of scientific inquiry and creative thought. Image streaming, developed by Win Wenger of the Institute for Visual Thinking, also builds self-confidence by providing a method for students to realize how much they know. The process encourages curiosity as students begin to wonder about the things they don't know.

For example: Ask students to find a partner. With eyes closed, one partner shares—for two minutes—everything he/she knows about the Arctic environment, including colors, land shapes, animals and people, temperature, light, sounds, the feel of the air, smells, and other sensory information. The imager is to speak continuously without stopping, simply allowing images and information to flow freely. The other person sits quietly and listens. After two minutes, change roles and allow the listener two minutes to image stream. Use the process to explore other environments (Africa, South America, the undersea world, outer space), travel vehicles, native peoples, or animals. It may be used for any other classroom topic as well.

Mind Maps

To synthesize the learning experience, create a mind map on the chalkboard. Put the topic in the center of a circle and ask students to share their images. Add them to the mind map to create a visual of the new information. Such mind maps make excellent study notes. (For a variety of examples, as well as instructions on making and using mind maps, see *Mapping Inner Space: Learning and Teaching Mind Mapping* by Nancy Margulies [Tucson, Ariz.: Zephyr Press, 1991].)

Activities: Exploring the Future

- Divide the class into four groups and create an expedition. As a class, decide on the expedition goal. Group one can describe in detail the environment the class will explore, including landforms, plants and animals, people who may live there, climate conditions, and dangers that may exist. This group may want to draw pictures or murals to illustrate the environment.

  Group two can plan the expedition: vehicles needed, number of people to take and the skills they need, food, clothing, shelter provisions, and new inventions needed. Make sure to determine how the money needed to pay for these items will be raised.

  Group three can create a scenario that details what happened on the expedition, including unexpected obstacles and how the explorers resolved the problems, new understandings gained, and what the explorers may have left behind. This may be written, illustrated, or acted out.

  Group four can create an account of the expedition that evaluates the success of the expedition, shares the important outcomes, places the exploration in historical context, and describes the effect of the expedition on the future of the land and people visited as well as the people who conducted the expedition. The account may be written, an illustrated documentary, a news or television program, a presentation by one of the explorers fifty years later, or a cassette recording.

- Sit quietly for a moment and reflect upon things you like to do. What are you most curious about? Make a mind map or list of your interests. Imagine yourself pursuing one of them. What would it feel like? How would you look? What might you need to develop or learn in order to accomplish your goal? Make a list of what you might need to do to prepare. Select two items from your list and do them.

- Think about the activities and skills your parents or other relatives have. How have they shared them with you? Do you find yourself interested in participating in their skills and interests? In what ways? If not, ask them if there is some way you can find out more about the things they like to do. Share your experiences with the class.

- Read a book about futuristics. What are the predictions for the world in the twenty-first century? What are the career fields that people may be involved in? Make a list and select one that intrigues you. Explore what is happening in the field right now. How can you become an explorer in that field and help to develop it? Write a report about the career and share your thoughts on your role as an explorer.

- With three other friends, create a clay city of the future. Include people in it and give it a name.

- Contact the Cousteau Society, NASA, the Smithsonian Institute, the Institute of Noetic Sciences, or another agency involved in explorations. Ask them what future expeditions they have planned. Share these plans with the class. Keep track of the progress of their explorations if you can.

- With the class, plan a field trip to an area you have never visited before. Consider it an expedition to find out something about the area, and write down your goals before you go. When you return, write an account of your exploration and what you feel you accomplished.

IV REFERENCE MATERIALS

Books marked with an asterisk are no longer in print but are valuable resources and may be available in some libraries or bookstores.

EXPLORATION

References for Children

Fradin, Dennis B. *Explorers.* Chicago: Childrens Press, 1984.
* Hale, John. *Age of Exploration.* Chicago: Time-Life, 1970.
Weiss, Harvey. *Maps: Getting from Here to There.* Boston: Houghton Mifflin, 1991.

References for Adults

Boorstin, David J. *The Discoverers: A History of Man's Search to Know His World and Himself.* New York: Random House, 1983.
* Doubleday and Company. *The Last Frontiers: The Encyclopedia of Discovery and Exploration.* New York: Doubleday, 1973.
Tourtellot, Jonathan B., ed. *Into the Unknown: The Story of Exploration.* Washington, D.C.: National Geographic, 1987.

COLUMBUS

References for Children

Adler, David A. *A First Biography: Christopher Columbus Great Explorer.* New York: Holiday House, 1991. (Grades 3–5)
Dyson, John. *Columbus: For Gold, God and Glory.* New York: Simon and Schuster, 1991.
Haskins, Jim. *Christopher Columbus, Admiral of the Ocean Sea.* New York: Scholastic, 1990. (Grades 5–8)
Leistman, Vicki. *Columbus Day.* Minneapolis: Carolrhoda Books, 1991. (Grades K–3)
Leon, George de Lucenary. *Explorers of the Americas Before Columbus.* New York: Franklin Watts, 1990. (Grades 7–9)

Levinson, Nancy S. *Christopher Columbus: Voyager to the Unknown.* New York: Lodestar, 1990. (Grades 4–8)

Maestro, Betsy, and Guilio Maestro. *The Discovery of the Americas.* New York: Lothrop, Lee, Shepard, 1991.

Meltzer, Milton. *Columbus and the World Around Him.* New York: Franklin Watts, 1990. (Grades 6 and up)

Roop, Peter, and Connie Roop, eds. *I, Columbus: My Journal, 1492–93.* New York: Avon Books, 1990.

Ventura, Piero. *Christopher Columbus.* New York: Random House, 1991.

References for Adults

Dor-Ner, Zvi. *Columbus and the Age of Discovery.* New York: William Morrow, 1991.

Fuson, Rebert H., trans. *The Log of Christopher Columbus.* Camden, Maine: International Marine, 1987.

Koning, Hans. *Columbus: His Enterprise.* New York: Monthly Review Press, 1991.

Sinovic, Vincent. *Columbus: Debunking of a Legend.* New York: Rivercross, 1990.

KINGSLEY

References for Children

* Hughes, Jean Gordon. *The Invincible Miss.* London: Macmillan, 1968.

* Syme, Ronald. *African Traveler: The Story of Mary Kingsley.* New York: William Morrow, 1962.

References for Adults

Frank, Katherine. *A Voyager Out: The Life of Mary Kingsley.* Boston: Houghton Mifflin, 1986.

* Howard, Cecil. *Mary Kingsley.* Hutchinson, 1957.

Kingsley, Mary. *Travels in West Africa: Congo francais, Corisco, and Cameroons.* Boston: Beacon Press, 1976.

———. *West African Studies.* F. Cass Publications, 1964.

* Wallace, Kathleen. *This Is Your Home: A Portrait of Mary Kingsley.* Portsmouth, N.H.: Heinemann, 1956.

AMUNDSEN

References for Children

Sipiera, Paul. *Roald Amundsen and Robert Scott: Race for the South Pole.* Chicago: Childrens Press, 1990. (Grades 3 and up)

References for Adults

* Amundsen, Roald. *My Life as an Explorer.* New York: Doubleday, 1928.
* ———. *The North-West Passage.* London: A. Constable, 1908.
* ———. *The South Pole: An Account of the Norwegian Antarctic Expedition in the* Fram. John Murray, 1912.
Amundsen, Roald, and Lincoln Ellsworth. *Two Against the Ice.* New York: Dodd, Mead, 1982.
Jackson, Donald Dale. *The Explorers.* Chicago: Time-Life, 1983.

COUSTEAU

References for Children

Greene, Carol. *Jacques Cousteau: Man of the Oceans.* Chicago: Childrens Press, 1990.
* Shannon, Terry. *Saucer in the Sea: The Story of the Cousteau Diving Saucer in Pacific Coast Waters.* San Carlos, California: Golden Gate Junior Books, 1965.
Simon, Seymour. *Oceans.* New York: William Morrow, Inc., 1990.
* Westman, Paul. *Jacques Cousteau: Free Flight Undersea.* Minneapolis: Dillon Press, 1980.

References for Adults

Cousteau, Jacques-Yves. *A Bill of Rights for Future Generations.* Myrin Institute, 1980. (Grades 8–12)
———. *The Silent World.* New York: Isis, 1989 (reprint).
* Cousteau, Jacques-Yves, and Philippe Diole. *Life and Death in a Coral Sea.* Garden City, New York: 1971.
Cousteau, Jacques-Yves, and James Dugan. *The Living Sea.* New York: Harper and Row, 1988.
———. *World without Sun.* New York: Harper and Row, 1964.
Cousteau, Jacques, and Alexis Sivirine. *Jacques Cousteau's* Calypso. New York: Harry N. Abrams, 1983.
Munson, Richard. *Cousteau: The Captain and His World.* New York: Paragon House, 1991.

OUTER SPACE

References for Children

Apfel, Necia H. *Voyager to the Planets.* New York: Clarion Books, 1991.

Asimov, Isaac. *The World's Space Programs.* Milwaukee: Gareth Stevens Children's Books, 1990.

* Black, Sonia, and Devra Newberger. *101 Outer Space Jokes.* New York: Scholastic, 1989.

Cole, Joanna. *The Magic School Bus: Lost in the Solar System.* New York: Scholastic., 1990.

Dolan, Edward F. *Famous Firsts in Space.* New York: EP Dutton, 1989.

Greenberg, Judith E. *Space.* Milwaukee: Raintree Publishers Limited Partnership, 1990.

* Irvine, Mat. *Understanding the Cosmos.* Morristown, New Jersey: Silver Burdett, 1986.

Kennedy, Gregory P. *The First Men in Space.* New York: Chelsea House, 1991.

Kerrod, Robin. *The All Color Book of Space.* New York: Arco, 1985.

Moche, Dinah L. *The Golden Book of Space Exploration.* New York: Golden, 1990.

* Poole, Gary. *Gag Galaxy: Outer Space Jokes and Riddles.* Tempo Books, 1980.

* Seymour, Simon. *Science at Work: Projects in Space Science.* New York: Franklin Watts, 1971. (check for revision SBN 531-01997)

Sullivan, George. *The Day We Walked on the Moon: A Photo History of Space Exploration.* New York: Scholastic, 1990.

Wood, Tim. *Out in Space.* New York: Aladdin Books, 1991.

References for Adults

Anzovin, Steve. *Our Future in Space.* New York: The H. W. Wilson Company, 1991. (Check for revision or update)

* Baker, David. *The History of Manned Space Flight.* New York: Crown Publishers, Inc. 1982.

* Moore, Patrick. *Travellers in Space and Time.* New York: Doubleday, 1984.

Shipman, Harry L. *Humans in Space: 21st Century Frontiers.* New York: Plenum Press, 1989.

OTHER MATERIALS

Calendar of Quincentenary events: Christopher Columbus. Quincentenary Jubilee Commission, 1801 F Street Northwest, Washington, D.C. 20006. 202-632-1992.

The Cousteau Society, 930 21st, Norfolk, VA 23517

Gueli, Lisa M., and Maria J. Scarapicchia. *The National Christopher Columbus Celebration Resource Handbook*. National Italian American Foundation.

NASA. *Discover Aeronautics and Space: A Coloring Book for Elementary Students.*

National Christopher Columbus Celebration, 666 11th Street NW Suite 800, Washington, DC 20001. 202-638-0220, 1992.

National Park Service, Dept. of the Interior. Directory of Columbus Quincentennial Projects. 1991 list of national parks with relevant education programs, exhibits, and national landmarks related to Columbus.

Tomb, Erik, and Nancy Conkle. *A Coloring Book of Great Explorers*. Santa Barbara, California: Bellerophon Books, 1987.

VIDEOCASSETTES

Exploring the Ocean Floor with Jacques Y. Cousteau. Barr Films, 1989. 24 minutes

Find Your Way Back: A Salute to the Space Shuttle. Cabin Fever Entertainment, 1989. 30 minutes

Pioneer of the Sea: Jacques Cousteau, the first 75 years. Turner Home Entertainment, 1990. 99 minutes

The Space Experience: Exploring the Edge. Cinema Guild, 1989. 26 minutes

Ten Who Dared: Mary Kingsley. Time-Life Multimedia, 1976. 52 minutes

Traveler's Tales. Films, Inc., 1980. 60 minutes

ADDITIONAL RESOURCES FROM ZEPHYR PRESS TO ENRICH YOUR PROGRAMS—

PHILOSOPHERS: Exploring Ideas through the Study of Six Great Lives

by Patton and Madigan (revised 1989)
Broaden your students' horizons by presenting some of the world's great philosophers—Buddha, Socrates, Thoreau, Gandhi, Rachel Carson, and Martin Luther King, Jr. Grades 5–12.
120 pages, 8 $\frac{1}{2}$" x 11", softbound.
ZS02-W . . . $14.95

MUSICIANS: Exploring Music through the Study of Six Great Lives

by Sally Patton (revised 1992)
This self-directed study unit introduces students to the elements of sound, instruments of the orchestra, elements of music, and six famous composers—Bach, Mozart, Beethoven, Debussy, Tchaikovsky, and Copland. Grades 2–6.
145 pages, 8 $\frac{1}{2}$" x 11", softbound.
ZS03-W . . . $14.95

REFLECTIONS ON WOMEN: Exploring Leadership through the Study of Five Great Lives

by Sally Patton (revised 1991)
Your students will not only research five exceptional women—Catherine the Great, Queen Victoria, Eleanor Roosevelt, Golda Meir, and Indira Gandhi—they'll also learn about monarchies and democracies from each woman's viewpoint. Grades 2–6.
68 pages, 8 $\frac{1}{2}$" x 11", softbound.
ZS08-W . . . $14.95

INVENTORS: Exploring Ingenuity through the Study of Five Great Lives

by Patton and Maletis (revised 1989)
Students examine the lives of Leonardo da Vinci, Benjamin Franklin, Thomas Edison, George Washington Carver, and the Wright brothers. Follow a time line of each inventor to find out how his creativity was affected by society and his environment. Grades 2–6.
72 pages, 8 $\frac{1}{2}$" x 11", softbound.
ZS01-W . . . $14.95

ARTISTS: Exploring Art through the Study of Five Great Lives

by Patton and Maletis (revised 1992)
Acquaint your students with the principles of design, the creative process, and five of the world's master artists—da Vinci, Homer, Picasso, Van Gogh, and Escher. Grades 2–6.
90 pages, 8 $\frac{1}{2}$" x 11", softbound.
ZS05-W . . . $14.95

Presenting the GREAT IDEAS SERIES—

ARCHITEXTURE: A Shelter Word

by Patton and Maxon (revised 1989)
Students explore our need for shelter as well as the influence of the environment and culture on the architecture of the world. Subtopics include—Caves, Pyramids, Homes of Ancient Greece, Castles, and Traditional Homes of Japan. Grades 2–6.
54 pages, 8 $\frac{1}{2}$" x 11", softbound.
ZS04-W . . . $14.95

ALPHABETICS: The History of Written Language

by Sally Patton (revised 1989)
This historical perspective of our alphabet encompasses the study of its major contributors—Prehistoric people, the Sumerians, the Egyptians, the Chinese, the Greeks, and the Romans. Grades 2–8.
92 pages, 8 $\frac{1}{2}$" x 11", softbound.
ZS06-W . . . $14.95

To order, write or call—

ZEPHYR PRESS
P.O. Box 13448-W
Tucson, Arizona 85732-3448
(602) 322-5090 • FAX (602) 323-9402

You can also request a free copy of our current catalog showing other learning materials that foster whole-brain learning, creative thinking, and self-awareness.